Paragraph

A Journal of Modern Critical Theory

Volume 43, Number 3, November 2020

Special Issue: New Takes on Film and Imagination

Edited by Sarah Cooper

Contents

New Takes on Film and Imagination

SARAH COOPER

When the nineteenth-century French poet Charles Baudelaire invites
his readers to go on a journey in one of his celebrated poems in
Les Fleurs du mal/The Flowers of Evil, transport comes by way of
imagination. The beauty, order and luxury, along with the calmness
and pleasures of the place to which this voyage takes us through the
alchemy of poetry that transforms base matter into gold, constitute a
paradise, albeit an ephemeral one.[1] Staying within a European context
and with poetry, if only for a while — we will soon venture far
further afield, forwards in time, and into film — the earlier writings
of the English Romantics William Wordsworth and Samuel Taylor
Coleridge were even more emphatic in valorizing the imagination.
Coleridge, in his version of a Kantian scheme, distinguished between
imagination that mediates between reason and understanding and
fancy that mediates between understanding and sense. He declared
imagination to be 'the living power and prime agent of all human
perception, and as a repetition of the finite mind of the eternal act of
creation in the infinite I AM'.[2] Coleridge the metaphysician contrasts
with the more grounded Wordsworth who never loses touch with
sensory evidence or nature, but for both poets imagination marks
out human beings as creators on the basis of the ability to form
mental images. 'My eyes make pictures, when they are shut', says
Coleridge, in 'A Day Dream', and in 'Lines Written a Few Miles
above Tintern Abbey', Wordsworth revisits the banks of the Wye
to describe how '[t]he picture of the mind revives again'.[3] Yet this
lauding of such imaginative wonder could not endure; indeed, less
celebratory attitudes towards the imagination already existed prior
to its Romantic heyday. The British empiricist Thomas Hobbes
characterized imagination as 'decaying sense'.[4] And that which Blaise
Pascal viewed as 'mistress of error and falsity'[5] always threatened to
dethrone its regal position as that Baudelairean 'queen of faculties'.[6]

Paragraph 43.3 (2020): 243–248
DOI: 10.3366/para.2020.0338
© Edinburgh University Press
www.euppublishing.com/para

In the twentieth century, imagination, the 'sovereign ghost', was no longer thought of as an essential power.[7] When Romantic poetry was addressed in literary criticism and theory, the object of praise was language rather than the individual poet as creator.[8] The blossoming of the imagination in Wordsworth and Coleridge, and its exquisite contortions through Baudelaire's flowers of evil, withers only to be deadheaded within the decidedly more barren Beckettian landscape of 'Imagination Dead Imagine'.[9] Apart from a resurgence of interest in lionizing the imagination on the part of Surrealists in the early twentieth century, what philosopher Richard Kearney has termed the postmodern turn from the image has involved a radical challenge ever since to the privileged position that imagination once occupied, and to its status as a separate faculty.[10] Within such terrain, and in the light of Kearney's observations, it may seem perverse to make imagination and imagining central topics here, especially in the image-based audiovisual context of film. But this volume sets out to showcase the role that film, film theory and film-philosophy are playing in stimulating renewed discussion of imagining and imagination today.

In contemporary film theory, cognitivist specialists have demonstrated the most sustained interest in imagination to date. Focusing on imagining and referring to 'the imagination' are not regressive gestures that seek to position the latter once again as a separate faculty but aim to recognize imagining as a fundamental aspect of mental activity. Cognitive theorists pioneered an earlier wave of scholarship on this topic within film studies, principally with reference to spectatorship. In the 1990s investigations into identification and mental simulation on the part of spectators (Gregory Currie) and the theorization of viewers as imaginative agents (Murray Smith) galvanized just some of the studies of imagining as a cognitive process.[11] This Special Issue acknowledges the inspiration of earlier cognitivist accounts and is not conceived as a complete break with them. It does however undertake to explore aspects of the relation between film and imagination that were not covered in that earlier research. Successive contributions open consideration of film and imagination to other theories and philosophies both within and beyond the Western context, in addition to engaging with a broad selection of filmmaking — narrative, art house, documentary and experimental — from around the world.

Many theorists and philosophers of imagination distinguish between cognitive imagining (conceptually entertaining a possibility) and sensory imagining (forming mental images), and it is the former that has received more attention within earlier accounts of spectatorial imagining. This volume begins otherwise by placing emphasis on sensory imagining. The image-making capacity of imagination — praised by Wordsworth and Coleridge — has been the subject of lengthy debate from the twentieth-century onwards, across philosophy and literary studies through different schools of psychology into neuroscience. So-called pictorialist or depictive theory came under attack in the mid-twentieth century in philosophy through the work of Jean-Paul Sartre, Gilbert Ryle and Ludwig Wittgenstein.[12] In earlier cognitivist studies, visualization and mental image-making were deemed largely irrelevant to spectatorial imagining.[13] In the opening article of this volume, Julian Hanich counters this view in his own research into the imagining or *mise en esprit* of what is omitted and only suggested, rather than represented, in film. Hanich attends to a recent cinematic trend towards the making of what he terms the 'one-character film', and his interest lies in those works that keep the viewer's sensory imagination constantly in play.

Key to Hanich's theorization of imagining on the spectator's part is an attention to sound. Albertine Fox's article further investigates the importance of sound in relation to spectatorship, focusing on Belgian director Chantal Akerman's documentary *South* (1999) and on the workings of imagination (and memory) from an auditory perspective. In her reading of this film, which centres on the racially motivated murder of the African American musician James Byrd Jr., Fox articulates a polyphonic mode of listening, attentive to sound and silence. She draws upon conceptions of imagination from Hannah Arendt and Toni Morrison to explore how spectators might see and imagine beyond racial binaries in order to access hidden voices and histories. Entwined throughout both Hanich's and Fox's articles is a dialogue between diverse theoretical and philosophical accounts of imagination, and the two subsequent articles continue this multifaceted exploration of spectatorial imagining.

Robert Sinnerbrink discusses various accounts of imagination — which he categorizes as phenomenological, cognitive, psychological and aesthetic — in order to outline his conception of 'perceptual imagining' and to put forwards a theory of embodied imagination, bridging the cognitive and sensory modes, and bringing out affective and corporeal aspects. He considers moreover the place of emotion in the discussion of spectatorship, arguing that emotional engagement and moral-ethical responsiveness work together in the experience of audiovisual narratives. He coins the term 'cinempathy' to speak to the interplay of empathy and sympathy involved in spectatorial responses to film. The ethical thrust of Sinnerbrink's argument intersects with a concern with the moral dimension in the subsequent article, too. Jane Stadler immerses us in Douglas Sirk's Hollywood melodrama *Imitation of Life* (1959) and continues discussion of spectatorship in an ethically nuanced way with particular reference to questions of race. Stadler puts forth an understanding of moral imagination, which couples a phenomenological perspective with neuroscientific research into embodied simulation and cognitive-philosophical approaches to film and art. While Stadler theorizes the spectator's imaginative involvement with the inner lives of onscreen characters, Sarah Cooper's ensuing interest lies in an engagement with flowers through the silent experimental work of Peruvian-born filmmaker Rose Lowder. Cooper's article attends to associations between beauty, imagination and the aesthetic in nature and art. She brings together the phenomenology of Sartre and Maurice Merleau-Ponty with writings on beauty, moral philosophy and feminist eco-philosophy, to consider Lowder's construction of perceptual-imaginative space and to explore how this involves spectators in an ethical-ecological perspective.

Already in Cooper's piece there is a shift away from thinking exclusively about spectatorial imaginative activity towards considering the construction of (perceptual-)imaginative space in film. Abraham Geil's article completes the move away from the spectator, still with interests in empathy and moral imagination that feature in Sinnerbrink's and Stadler's articles, but transferring this now to an association between imagination and film form. Reconceptualizing empathy as a problematic of form rather than psychological experience, Geil peruses the imaginary terrain of the face in film. He traces the genealogy of empathy (*Einfühlung*) in German aesthetics, engaging critically with this concept to make contrasting readings of '#Look Beyond Borders', an online video produced by Amnesty International, and documentaries by Dutch filmmaker Johan van der Keuken from the 1960s and the 1990s. Geil's fascination with form leads into the next article where imagination is charted through the aesthetic space of the image.

Saige Walton takes up Gaston Bachelard's extensive philosophical writings on imagination in order to account for the workings of imagination in Hungarian director Ildikó Enyedi's *Testről és lélekről/ On Body and Soul* (2017). Walton's interest in the scope of imagination as it relates to the human and non-human animal as well as the surrounding natural world in Enyedi's film follows Bachelard's elemental and material concerns, as she extends the connection between imagination and form that Geil's contribution inaugurated. Walton's Bachelardian reading draws specifically on his conception of vertical time, and she relates this to the temporality of dreams in Enyedi's film. The final contribution to the volume also refers us to dreams. Victor Fan explores the relationship between imaging and imagining in cinema through the lens of Buddhism, showing how these processes bridge inner and outer worlds, and revealing the dreamlike and illusory status of all phenomena, as well as their impermanence, even as we regard them as existent and perceive them as continuous. He exemplifies his discussion with Chinese director Bi Gan's film *Diqiu zuihou de yewan/Long Day's Journey into Night* (2018).

Journeying from consideration of image formation in the spectator's mind to the forms and aesthetics of imagination on screen, and from questions of embodied spectatorship to connections to the non-human, material and elemental, the articles gathered here present divergent takes on the relation between film and imagination, yet all are united in recognizing its richness as a topic for current and future research.

NOTES

1 'L'Invitation au voyage' in Charles Baudelaire, *Les Fleurs du mal et autres poèmes* (Paris: Garnier-Flammarion, 1964 [1857]), 77–8.
2 Samuel Taylor Coleridge, *Biographia Literaria* (London: CreateSpace Independent Publishing Platform, 2014 [1817]), 62.
3 'A Day Dream' in Samuel Taylor Coleridge, *The Golden Book of Coleridge* (New York: E. P. Dutton and Co., 1895), 193; 'Lines Written a Few Miles above Tintern Abbey on Revisiting the Banks of the Wye during a Tour, July 13, 1798' in William Wordsworth, *Selected Poems* (London: Penguin, 2004), 63.
4 Thomas Hobbes, *Leviathan* (Oxford: Oxford University Press 2008 [1651]), 11.
5 Blaise Pascal, *Pensées*, translated by W. F. Trotter (New York: E. P. Dutton and Co., 1958 [1670]), 24.
6 Charles Baudelaire, 'Salon de 1859' [1859] in *Écrits sur l'art* (Paris: Librairie Générale Française, 1992), 243–321 (257).
7 Denis Donoghue, *The Sovereign Ghost: Studies in Imagination* (New York: Ecco Press, 1976).
8 See I. A. Richards, *Coleridge on Imagination* (Kegan Paul: London, 1934).
9 'Imagination Dead Imagine' [1965] in Samuel Beckett, *The Complete Short Prose 1929–1989* (London: Grove Press, 1997), 182–5. The piece was

translated into French and included as part of *Têtes-mortes* (Paris: Minuit, 1967), 49–57.

10 Richard Kearney, *The Wake of Imagination* (London: Routledge, 1988), 9.

11 Gregory Currie, *Image and Mind: Film, Philosophy, and Cognitive Science* (Cambridge: Cambridge University Press, 1995) and Murray Smith, *Engaging Characters: Fiction, Emotion, and the Cinema* (Oxford: Oxford University Press, 1995).

12 For an overview of the extensive scholarship on mental imagery, see Nigel J. T. Thomas, 'Mental Imagery' in *The Stanford Encyclopaedia of Philosophy* (Fall 2014 Edition), edited by Edward N. Zalta, http://plato.stanford.edu/archives/fall2014/entries/mental-imagery/, consulted 11 February 2020.

13 This differs from the resurgence of interest in mental image-making in the literary sphere: see, for example, Elaine Scarry, *Dreaming by the Book* (Princeton: Princeton University Press, 1999). For discussion of film spectatorship and the experience of mental image-making, see Sarah Cooper, *Film and the Imagined Image* (Edinburgh: Edinburgh University Press, 2019).

Mise en Esprit: One-Character Films and the Evocation of Sensory Imagination

JULIAN HANICH

What is a One-Character Film?

Over the last decade we have witnessed a remarkable cinematic trend: the flourishing of narrative feature films relying on a single onscreen character. These one-character films, as I will simply call them, have precursors that reach back at least to the 1960s. Yet it is in the 2010s that we can observe a particularly strong propensity among filmmakers in showing only one character on the screen. Far from necessarily a-cinematic or theatrical, one-character films can epitomize the virtues of a sophisticated filmic simplicity, as if to lend credence to an aphorism once quipped by Friedrich Wilhelm Murnau: 'Real art is simple, but simplicity requires the greatest art.'[1] Although my inventory is most likely shot through with gaps (just witness the strong bias towards English-language films), I have examples like the following in mind:

- *Yaadein* (1964, by Sunil Dutt, with himself as the only actor);[2]
- *The Human Voice* (1966, by Ted Kotcheff, with Ingrid Bergman) and other adaptations of Cocteau's *La Voix humaine* such as *Die geliebte Stimme* (1960) with Hildegard Knef;
- *Un homme qui dort/The Man Who Sleeps* (1974, by Georges Perec/Bernard Queysanne, with Jacques Spiesser);
- *The Noah* (1975, by Daniel Bourla, with Robert Strauss);
- *Give 'em Hell, Harry!* (1975, by Steven Binder/Peter H. Hunt, with James Whitmore);
- *Brontë* (1983, by Delbert Mann, with Julie Harris);
- *Secret Honor* (1984, by Robert Altman, with Philip Baker Hall);

Paragraph 43.3 (2020): 249–264
DOI: 10.3366/para.2020.0339
© Edinburgh University Press
www.euppublishing.com/para

- *Missing Link* (1988, by Carol and David Hughes, with Peter Elliott);
- *Krapp's Last Tape* (2000, by Atom Egoyan, with John Hurt) and other adaptations of Beckett's monodrama;
- *Buried* (2010, by Rodrigo Cortés, with Ryan Reynolds);
- *Locke* (2013, by Steven Knight, with Tom Hardy);
- *All is Lost* (2013, by J. C. Chandor, with Robert Redford);
- *Nightingale* (2014, by Elliott Lester with David Oyelowo);
- *Kollektor/Collector* (2016, by Alexey Krasovsky, with Konstantin Khabensky);
- *Den Skyldige/The Guilty* (2018, by Gustav Möller, with Jakob Cedergren);
- *Arctic* (2019, by Joe Penna, with Mads Mikkelsen).[3]

Of course, crafting a new category is risky business and might raise eyebrows. Therefore a number of caveats seem necessary. First, I categorize films like *The Man Who Sleeps*, *The Guilty* and *Arctic* as one-character films, even though they contain brief appearances of other persons and feature short interactions. However, in all three cases the bit parts are negligibly small; in fact, the persons encountered by the character resemble background props more than supporting characters with agency. Second, I see no reason to distinguish between films with a theatrical release and movies made for television like ABC's *The Human Voice* or HBO's *Nightingale*. Third, I have deliberately put emphasis on the term 'character', because I focus exclusively on narrative fiction films. Thus, one-*person* avant-garde films like Andy Warhol's *Sleep* (1963, with John Giorno) and Thierry Zéno's *Vase de noces* (1974, with Dominique Garny), documentaries with one protagonist like Kim Ki-duk's *Arirang* (2011, with himself as the only one onscreen) or experimental-documentary hybrids such as Romuald Karmakar's *Das Himmler-Projekt* (2000, with Manfred Zapatka) fall outside of my scope. The same goes for filmed one-person stage performances like Jonathan Demme's *Swimming to Cambodia* (1987, with Spalding Gray). This decision is somewhat arbitrary, but it will allow a more focused analysis. Suffice it to say that a number of my observations below may also illuminate the discussion of non-fictional one-person films.

Finally, I have qualified the term 'one-character film' with a reference to a character *onscreen*. This qualification is important because some of the most striking one-character films feature protagonists that are present via telecommunication devices but remain absent onscreen;

throughout the film these offscreen characters appear only as *acousmatic voices*, to use Michel Chion's well-known term. Thus, depending on how strictly one defines one-character films, some of the above-mentioned films do not fully qualify. In the end it might therefore be more useful to endorse prototype theory: some one-character films (say *Secret Honor* or *All is Lost*) are more prototypical than others (such as *The Guilty* or *Arctic*).

Yet, and this further emphasizes the trend and encourages me to investigate the category, over and above one-character films narrowly defined we come across an astonishing number of critically acclaimed and/or financially successful films that focus on a single character for a major part of their screen time. Following precursors like *Silent Running* (1972, by Douglas Trumbull, with Bruce Dern) we could think of *Cast Away* (2000, by Robert Zemeckis, with Tom Hanks), *I Am Legend* (2007, by Francis Lawrence, with Will Smith), *127 Hours* (2010, by Danny Boyle, with James Franco), *Life of Pi* (2012, by Ang Lee, with Suraj Sharma), *Gravity* (2013, by Alfonso Cuarón, with Sandra Bullock) and *The Shallows* (2016, by Jaume Collet-Serra, with Blake Lively). In these films the supporting characters either get lost along the way, appear only later in the film, feature in parts that frame an extended one-character section or flare up in memory flashbacks throughout the film. In some cases the one-character section comes close to or even exceeds the screen time of fully fledged one-character films: think of the roughly eighty minutes Tom Hanks has by himself in *Cast Away* or the sixty minutes reserved for Suraj Sharma as the only human character in *Life of Pi*.

Naturally, the one-character film is not without precursors. At least three forerunners have influenced its form. First, the one-character film can be seen as a continuation and radicalization of the *chamber film*, as developed in Germany in the 1920s, with the Carl-Mayer-written films *Scherben/Shattered* (1921) and *Sylvester/New Year's Eve* (1924) as prime examples. Recently, Thomas J. Connelly discussed it under the term 'cinema of confinement' and grouped together films that primarily take place in one setting like *Phone Booth* (2002) or *10 Cloverfield Lane* (2016).[4] I speak of a 'radicalization' of the chamber film because one-character films not only further limit the cast, but in cases like *Locke* or *The Guilty* also play out in real time, thus taking the call of the chamber film for unity of time quite literally. Moreover, the one-character film bears resemblance to the *monodrama* in theatre with its rich tradition since Rousseau's *Pygmalion* (1762) and Goethe's *Proserpina* (1777).[5] In fact, a number of one-character films are adaptations of theatrical monodramas — think of Kotcheff's *La Voix humaine/The Human Voice*, Egoyan's *Krapp's Last Tape* or Altman's rendering of the stage play *Secret Honor*. Finally, at least in one of its subtypes the one-character film comes close to and is influenced by the *radio drama* and its popular successor, the *narrative podcast*. This is literally true for Delbert Mann's *Brontë* with Julie Harris, based on William Luce's 1979 radio play *Currer Bell, Esq.* Yet it is more formally the case in those films that will eventually emerge as the main focus of this essay — what I call *centrifugal* one-character films.

One-character films know a broad spectrum. It ranges from (a) extremely laconic films entirely focused on the action in the narrative here-and-now like *All is Lost* and *Missing Link* where what we get is what we see and even backstories of the solitary characters remain sparse, via (b) highly talkative films that revolve around soliloquies of self-reflection, questioning of identity and a problematizing of the narrative past such as *Secret Honor* and *Krapp's Last Tape* to (c) dialogue-heavy films that — via phones and other telecommunication devices — reach far beyond the depicted scene. In films such as *The Guilty* and *Locke* much of the action does not take place *hic-et-nunc* (here-and-now) but rather *ibi-et-nunc* (there-and-now). While the former do not raise any questions about what goes on elsewhere, in the latter these questions loom large. These films therefore *centrifugally* thrust us into a simultaneous present that remains invisible.

To put it in a somewhat simplified way: the first group of films places its emphasis on *actions*, the second group focuses on *words*, and the third group revolves around *actions-through-words*. While in the first case we are observers of acting characters and in the second we follow them talking, in the third case we observe characters observing. Or better: we observe them listening to the actions and words of others to which they react with words. In terms of influence the first group of one-character films comes closest to the chamber film, the second to the stage monodrama and the third to the radio play.

Alternatively, however, we may also treat these three tendencies as modes or registers *within* a given one-character film: most one-character films smoothly shift registers, even while retaining an overall emphasis on one of the three modes. This may ultimately prove more productive for analysis, also because one-character films can be centrifugal in various temporal forms: they can catapult us not only into a present elsewhere, but also, via messenger reports, into the past or, via character speeches, into the future. Moreover, the degrees of

Figure 1. Asger Holm (Jakob Cedergren) in *Den Skyldige/The Guilty* (2018) by Gustav Möller

Figure 2. Paul Conroy (Ryan Reynolds) in Rodrigo Cortés' *Buried* (2010)

centrifugality can vary substantially *between* films and *within* a film, depending on how evocative and suggestive the 'other end of the line' is and hence how vividly the film plays with the viewer's imagination. A film like *The Guilty* (Figure 1) constantly changes its scope, as if expanding and shrinking: during the phone conversations it moves far away from the emergency call centre in which it takes place and comes back to it in moments when we see protagonist Asger Holm (Jakob Cedergren) getting up and going to the water cooler or having a brief conversation with his colleague.

Or consider *Buried* (Figure 2): protagonist Paul Conroy (Ryan Reynolds), taken hostage and held captive in a coffin in the Iraqi desert, needs to solve a series of problems of how to survive (a most popular theme in many one-character films). He has to get rid of his gag and bonds, retrieve a cell phone or fight a snake that has sneaked into his coffin. Besides such displays of physical actions and skilful coping with obstacles, Conroy leads numerous phone conversations with his mother-in-law, a nasty clerk from his company, and so on. However, compared to the strong suggestiveness of many telephone dialogues in *The Guilty*, these conversations focus much less on the actions at the other end of the line but on what the persons tell Conroy to do in the here and now. Yet *Buried*, too, occasionally switches into a centrifugal mode and confronts us with moments in which actions are merely suggested through words and sound effects.

Halfway through the film, Conroy calls a nursing home and requests to speak to his mother. The filtered voice of the nurse answers: 'Um, okay. Let me bring the cordless phone to her room. Hold on one moment please.' We hear footsteps in a hallway and a creaking door. Then the nurse, now somewhat remote from the receiver, says: 'Mrs. Conroy, you have a telephone call, dear. Here, you can use this phone.' While the camera stays with Conroy in close-up, the action verbs 'bring' and 'use', the descriptive noun 'cordless phone' as well as sound effects of walking and door-opening allow us to imagine — more or less vividly — what is going on in the nursing home. What happens to the viewer is a shift of reception mode typical of centrifugal one-character films: a stronger emphasis on *listening* to the detriment of seeing and a heightened focus on *imagination* at the cost of perception.

As these examples indicate, one-character films can strongly toy with the viewers' *sensory imagination*. More specifically, they can make us *mentally visualize* by referring, in clever ways, to absent spaces and actions, thus enabling an experience of 'mental superimposition' or 'mental double-exposure': the audiovisual perception of the film is enriched and layered-on-top with sensory imagination of the visual kind. While we *see* only one character, we are invited to *imagine* an entire cast that remains invisible. To be sure, the vividness of sensory imagination varies between individuals: some persons imagine much more strongly than others. Those who do imagine — if only mildly — will likely feel sent centrifugally beyond the film frame into an imaginary elsewhere. Coining a new term we could claim that the *mise en scène* is enriched by — and embedded in — a *mise en esprit*. The plots ostensibly take place in nothing but a car, a police office or a coffin underground, but we have to transcend the boundaries of the location and move into an imagined scenery evoked by voices and sounds. We negotiate, in other words, between the on-seen and the off-sent.

It is for this reason that I propose to locate at least some one-character films squarely within the aesthetic tradition I have dubbed 'omission, suggestion, completion': these films deliberately *omit* parts of the action and merely *suggest* what happens so that viewers mentally *complete* what has been left out.[6] Since what the viewer imaginatively fills in is often rich and detailed and involves various bodily registers — for instance visual imagination — it would be wrong to think of centrifugal one-character films as 'austere', 'abstract' or 'ascetic'. While we may talk about an aesthetics of 'absence', 'restriction' or 'simplicity' (as I have done above), the often-used term 'minimalist' is convincing only in an economic sense but does not describe the viewer's varied aesthetic experience.

I am particularly interested in how centrifugal one-character films derive their dramatic tension from keeping the viewer's sensory imagination busy. And imagine they do: we can retrieve abundant evidence from user comments on IMDb, film reviews in newspapers and magazines as well as directors' commentaries. Jeannette Catsoulis, for one, writes in the *New York Times*: 'the stripped-down Danish thriller *The Guilty* paints such vivid pictures with words that, afterward, we're not exactly sure what we saw and what was merely imagined.'[7] The director of *Locke*, Steven Knight, himself reports that 'One of the best things people say to me afterward is they forget they haven't seen the other characters. They do it themselves.'[8] Of course, these comments only testify *that* sensory imagining occurred, but not through what means it was evoked and how it was experienced. These aspects will be the goal of the rest of my essay.

How to Evoke the Viewer's Sensory Imagination

First, we need to clarify how we designate the space we mentally fill in. Are we dealing with a lateral ellipsis here — that is, a spatial rather than temporal omission in which an important narrative element is spatially circumnavigated and conspicuously left aside?[9] In a previous essay I have proposed to speak of a lateral ellipsis only if there are *no* direct sensual suggestions of what remains absent.[10] Since there are abundant aural cues in centrifugal one-character films, it is better to resort to the term 'offscreen space'. However, offscreen space is not a well-defined term, as Chion pointed out a long time ago. Pertinently for our case, he asks: 'where should we situate sounds (usually voices) that come from electrical devices located in the action and that the image suggests or directly shows: telephone receivers, radios, public-address speakers?'[11] I therefore suggest distinguishing between the *immediate off* and the *medial off*.[12] The immediate off refers to offscreen space more or less directly beyond the film frame and within the range of normal sense perception of the characters (thus covering the six segments of offscreen space defined by Noël Burch); the medial off includes those parts of offscreen space we have aural or visual access to *via media* but which are located far beyond the immediate off.

Usually, what brings into play this medial off in one-character films are telecommunication devices like the cell phone, the walkie-talkie or the hands-free kit which connect the protagonist to the offscreen personage. But how to mark off this invisible personage if we want to avoid the term 'character'? With Chion we might call the protagonist the *proxi-locutor* and the latter the *tele-locutor*.[13] (Of course, the mere use of a telephone call does not guarantee a strong centrifugal tendency, as the adaptations of Cocteau's *La Voix humaine* and the many telephone scenes in *Nightingale* make clear, where we aurally stay with the protagonist and do not hear what the tele-locutor says in the medial off.)

It is precisely in this medial off where a lot of the action takes place, but it is in our embodied minds where we have to actualize and concretize it. When in *The Guilty* Asger Holm presses a button to take his next emergency call, a new filmic world elsewhere suddenly seems to open its gates. It magnetizes our attention — at least in parts — away from Asger and his emergency desk and we begin to 'mentally look' into that space beyond. It's an acousmatic world of voices and sound effects to which we have no visual access, a *mise en esprit* which gradually takes shape in our mind through acoustic information. But just as the *mise en scène* can be densely packed or rarefied, so can the *mise en esprit* be plastic or vague. Moreover, the conversations between proxi- and tele-locotur can open up far-reaching deep worlds or they can remain small and flat and close to the unseen interlocutor on the phone. In his phenomenology of the radio drama Friedrich Knilli has introduced a distinction between plays that make listeners evoke an entire scene (*Szenenstücke*) and plays that conjure up predominantly persons (*Personenstücke*). While the former include the entire world of things, the latter restrict themselves almost exclusively to the tele-locutors.[14] This distinction is also useful for how the medial off takes shape in our mind: as mentioned above, a film like *Buried* hardly ever leaves the confines of the 'person piece', while *The Guilty* goes to great lengths to evoke entire scenes.

But what are preconditions and causes that allow films to make viewers populate and furnish a well-defined *mise en esprit* through mental visualizations and other forms of sensory imagination? The following list ranges from mere facilitating factors (point a) to catalysts of mental visualizations (points b–d).

a) Reduced within-modality interference
In comparison to reading a literary text or listening to a radio play, the film spectator is in a disadvantaged position when it comes to visually imagining what is not shown. Visually, the reader of a literary text is merely confronted with what Anežka Kuzmičová calls the decoding of 'flat monochrome signs on a page', an activity that 'does not necessarily have to interfere, or not too strongly, with mental imagery'.[15] The listener to the radio drama can look at an unmoving background like a wall or even close his or her eyes altogether to focus on the act of imagining.[16] The film spectator, on the other hand, usually follows what is shown onscreen with his or her sense of sight and therefore might run the risk of what cognitive scientists call 'within-modality interference'. As Kuzmičová explains: 'Within-modality interference (. . .) entails that mental imaging in a given sensory modality becomes more difficult if a physical stimulus is simultaneously present in the same modality.'[17] Neuroscientists assume that the negative effect of visual activity on mental visualization derives from the involvement of the same brain regions in vision and visual imagination because both have common neural substrates.[18] In other words, to visualize mentally while watching a film might be cognitively taxing — unless the filmmaker takes precautions and lessens the cognitive visual load. This is why directors often use long takes to avoid the abrupt shifts in perspective and other visual distractions that come with editing. Similarly, the camera remains either static or the mobile frame is reduced to slow pans or zooms. Not least, the *mise en scène* is freed of attention-grabbing content, most notably because we are dealing with stationary characters lying in a coffin, driving a car or sitting at a desk.

While involved in — what for the viewer are meant to be imagination-igniting — conversations, these characters often look captivated and focused into off-screen space.[19] It is as if these characters were trying to imagine what is happening at the other end of the line, thus allowing us to switch into the mode of imagining ourselves. Here unobtrusive acting often dominates as well: in *The Guilty* and *Locke* the characters have emotional outbursts only *between* the conversations. Finally, scientific studies have shown that mental visualizations suffer in brightly illuminated spaces — visual imagination, in other words, functions best in the dark.[20] This confirms the strategy of filmmakers to situate their one-character films in dark environments. Here the barely illuminated coffin in *Buried* — essentially a 95-minute exercise in chiaroscuro lighting — serves as a case in point. Similarly, *Locke* and *The Guilty* not only take place at night, but the latter also finds narrative motivation for creating imagination-conducive conditions for the viewer: the more intense the narrative, the darker the surroundings.

b) Suggestive verbalizations

The reduced within-modality-interference is a mere facilitating factor, but it does not ignite sensory imagination itself. It helps to free cognitive resources and allows us to glide smoothly from perception-controlled viewing into a mode of spectatorship dominated by imagining. For a strong catalyst of mental visualization we have to move on to 'suggestive verbalizations'. With this term I designate particularly plastic, vivid language that invites, challenges, even forces a viewer to imagine in a visual, aural, olfactory, gustatory or tactile way something that is not shown — language that enables the viewer to make present to him- or herself the non-present in a sensory way. In order to evoke linguistically what remains absent all kinds of language can be brought into play.[21]

For example, at the beginning of *The Guilty* we hear a man calling from his cell phone, cars are passing by in the background, rain is falling. The man explains that he has just been mugged and that he is sitting in his car: 'A woman pulled a knife and took my wallet and computer — which contains work I need.' Asger asks him if this had happened on the street. 'No, as I said, in my car!' the man replies. These brief snippets may be enough to elicit a relatively clearly defined visualization of the man's environment and what happened during the mugging. But the dialogue furnishes the *mise en esprit* with further brief descriptions of persons and props, like the man's blue BMW. When Asger asks how the woman looked, the man answers: 'She was young. Dark hair.' — 'Danish?' — 'No, more…' — 'Eastern European?'– 'Yes.'

In recent years cognitive scientists and literary scholars have made considerable headway in identifying types of language encouraging mental visualizations and other forms of sensory imagination. One major lesson is that the principle of 'the more descriptive detail, the better' can lead to cognitive overload.[22] In contrast, the narration of *simple, bodily actions* easily prompts the reader or listener to visualize. This is especially true if these bodily actions are *volitional* and *goal-oriented*.[23] In centrifugal one-character films we can find various narratively motivated scenes with character speeches containing purposive bodily actions, precisely because the characters have to give instructions to their tele-locutors. For instance, Ivan Locke at one point calls his son to retrieve an item for him: 'In my blue coat in the kitchen, yes? There's a notebook. There's a phone number in the notebook of somebody called Cassidy who works for the council clerk of works. I need the number.'

In addition, these *imperatives* to execute simple, bodily actions — which also function as implicit calls to the viewer to imagine — often include either explicitly or implicitly the objects on which the tele-locutors have to act and the affordances of these objects. This is helpful for imagining because, as Kuzmičová adds, language becomes particularly imagination-friendly if it includes *transitive movements* — that is, movements that involve physical objects. What is more, the transitive movements are best directed at *everyday artefacts* whose affordances are well known.[24] In a dialogue between Ivan Locke and his assistant, Donal, Locke's brief imperatives not only explicitly mention everyday objects (pen, drawer, folder), but also include implicit descriptions of how to act on what these objects afford (for instance, opening a drawer by grabbing its handle and pulling it).

But centrifugal dialogue passages do not only play out in the form of imperatives, but they may also follow a *question-and-answer model*. This seems highly conducive to mental visualizations because questions imply retarding moments that raise curiosity. The most harrowing scene in *The Guilty*, for instance, is shot through with questions, answered by brief suggestive verbalizations, as when Asger, on the phone, asks a colleague about the state of a four-year-old girl: 'I don't know, but she has blood on her hands and blouse.'

c) The acousmatic voice

What the voice from the medial off describes is arguably the single most crucial factor for how we imagine the *mise en esprit*. But, as Don Ihde reminds us, '*What is* said, the discursive, in voice is never present alone but is amplified within the possibilities of *how* the voice says it.'[25] Particularly, in 'person pieces' that remain focused on the tele-locutors and do not provide much further visualizable information, but also in those moments of 'scene pieces' when the evocative power of the linguistic content recedes, the voice itself carries evocative force. First of all, the voice can lend a — however vague — visual quality to the tele-locutor as a person *in general*. This is certainly true in terms of gender and age. But in combination with narrative content and through dialect, sociolect or accent we can often also infer regional background and social class, which might elicit idiosyncratic (visual) connotations for each viewer. For instance, from the hoarse voice of Iben, the woman in *The Guilty* allegedly abducted by her husband, one could deduce that she is either a heavy smoker or drinker or both and that this might qualify her as a member of the lower class.

But on top of these *general* qualities of the tele-locutor, the modulated voice also allows us to visualize *momentary* facial expressions and bodily postures that come with emotions or altered physiological states: the angry shout, the sad cry, the scared scream, the startled exclamation, the derisive laughter, the slurred voice of a person who drank too much — these invisible vocal expressions may also come with a visualizable quality.

Again, I do not claim that we necessarily have very plastic visualizations of the tele-locutors, nor that we always imagine them in detail. As Zenon Pylyshyn exemplifies: 'I often feel I have a vivid image of someone's face, but when asked whether the person wears glasses, I find that my image is silent on that question: it neither has nor lacks glasses, (. . .) nor does it contain the information that something is missing.'[26] Quoting Ned Block, Emily Troscianko calls this feature of our imagination 'inexplicitly noncommittal'.[27] But indeterminacy is not an argument against the occurrence of mental visualizations per se. In fact, the phenomenon Chion calls *de-acousmatization* — when the acousmatic voice is finally endowed with a face and the viewer gets to see the previously invisible character — often comes with a (however mild) rupture because the acousmatic voice had evoked a different visual expectation.[28]

d) Sound effects

'[T]he shortest, simplest sound can conjure up an entire scene, if it is charged clearly and sufficiently with unequivocal associations. For example: any dull thud is indefinite, but the sound of a champagne glass is unmistakable,' Rudolf Arnheim writes.[29] Sound effects are a vital factor for igniting the viewer's imagination, and they come in various forms:

1. *Immediately recognizable sounds*: this is the term Chion uses for sounds that are clearly and irrefutably identified, at least by persons belonging to a particular community or demographic, such as trains, cars, horses, dogs, seagulls, police sirens, rain drops, church bells, footsteps, slammed doors and so on.[30] For instance, in the harrowing child scene from *The Guilty* the sound effects from the medial off comprise footsteps of various speeds and creaking doors.
2. *Keynotes*: According to R. Murray Schafer, keynotes are background sounds not listened to consciously but connected to specific societies or locales which they might evoke, such as foghorns connected to port towns. For instance, in *Buried* we can hear — from the immediate (not the medial) off the stereotypical sound of a muezzin singing — which may evoke a sun-flooded, dry Arab countryside.
3. *Materializing sound indices*: this is Chion's technical term for those aspects of sound that make us realize the material nature of its source and how they were emitted: they not only inform about the substance causing the sound (wood, metal, paper) but also how the sound is produced (by friction, impact, periodic movement back and forth).[31] In the nursing home scene from *Buried*, we can hear female footsteps that evoke high-heels walking on a tiled floor in an empty hallway. Thus, they give away much more sound indices — and hence are more visualizable — than the rather abstract footsteps in *The Guilty*.

Sound effects can also evoke spatial dimensions and dynamics in rather concrete ways through factors like depth, distance, direction and reverberation. Think of the aforementioned depth of the medial off: are we dealing with a flat versus a deep scene, a scene that remains close to the tele-locutor or that opens up a world beyond him or her? Volume and the pitching and filtering of the actor's voice can indicate if a person is close to the telecommunication device or standing far away, if she is moving away from it or towards it (remember, again, the nursing home scene from *Buried*). The scene can also be layered, include a foreground and a background and shift the focus from fore- to background and vice versa. Not least, reverberation or lack of echo can indicate something about the extension of space (in *Buried* the effect of being situated in an empty nursing home corridor derives from the strong reverberation in this scene).[32]

Director Gustav Moeller uses particularly evocative sound effects in a scene with a quasi-live character some sixteen minutes into *The Guilty* — it's as if we were listening to the broadcast of an O. J. Simpson-like car chase on a freeway. We see Asger Holm tensely listening to the report of a colleague in a police patrol car on the freeway heading north of Copenhagen through the rain and at high speed in order to find an abducted victim. From the medial off we can hear the patrol car's engine and the sound of cars passing. Again, the centrifugal dialogue largely follows a question-and-answer structure. At first the policemen seem to lose the vehicle, but then they turn on their sirens and close in on a white van. We can hear the car stop, the engine turned off, a voice in the background. With the line open, the policemen leave the car. The nearest sounds are from the windshield wipers in the patrol car, which keep moving throughout the scene, but we also hear footsteps whose volume decreases and which are gradually moving away from the car. In the background we hear the voice of one man screaming 'Police. Let me see your hands. Keep them on the wheel.' Again footsteps, screams in the background, noise from the walkie-talkie and so on.

Centrifugal one-character films like *The Guilty* thus allow for a refocused attention to the aural world and, more specifically, the onscreen and offscreen human voice. While early champions of the visual close-up — from Béla Balázs to Fritz Lang — dreamed of a 'rediscovery' of the human face, one-character films offer an intricate interplay and 'rediscovery' of the human face *and* the human voice as well as a sensory confrontation between two forms of actor's performance: an audiovisual, full-bodied one versus an auditory, voiced-based one. Simultaneously, centrifugal one-character films enable an aesthetic experience suspended between what Chion calls *visualized* listening (where we see the sound source) and *acousmatic* listening (where the sound source remains invisible), between *audio-vision* (where the image is the centre of attention to which sound adds value) and *visio-audition* (where the auditory part is focused on and the image merely adds to it), between *watching* a film and *imagining* the rest of it. No doubt, for many viewers this elicits deep pleasure: discovering the potency of film as a medium of mental visualizations and a foregrounding of sensory imagination.

NOTES

1   Quoted from Graham Petrie, *Hollywood Destinies: European Directors in America, 1922–1931*, revised edition (Detroit: Wayne State University Press, 2001), 74.

2   I did not have a chance to see *Yaadein*, but its opening credits reportedly describe it as the 'World's First One-Actor Movie', https://scroll.in/reel/832009/rajkummar-rao-isnt-the-only-one-who-is-trapped-he-shares-his-agonywith-sunil-dutt-in-yaadein, consulted 14 August 2019.

3   Apart from feature films we can find single characters also in short films (Mike Leigh's *A Sense of History* from 1992, with Jim Broadbent), as part of an omnibus film ('Una voce umana' from Roberto Rossellini's 1948 *L'Amore*, with Anna Magnani) or in television series (the 2015 'Heaven Sent' episode from the ninth season of *Doctor Who*, with Peter Capaldi).

4   Thomas J. Connelly, *Cinema of Confinement* (Evanston: Northwestern University Press, 2019). Many one-character films are one-location dramas, sometimes even restricted to a single room or even a coffin as in the case of *Buried*. But in *The Man Who Sleeps* or *Missing Link* this is not the case. Additionally, moving vehicles — like the car on the freeway in *Locke* or the ship on the Indian Ocean in *All is Lost* — complicate our understanding of what a single location means.

5   On the theatrical monodrama, see A. Dwight Culler, 'Monodrama and the Dramatic Monologue', *PMLA* 90:3 (1975), 366–85.

6   Julian Hanich, 'Omission, Suggestion, Completion: Film and the Imagination of the Spectator', *Screening the Past* 43 (2018), n.p.

7   https://www.nytimes.com/2018/10/18/movies/the-guilty-review.html, consulted 14 August 2019.

8   https://www.latimes.com/entertainment/movies/moviesnow/la-et-mn-locke-20140425-story.html, consulted 14 August 2019. Or take this IMDb entry on *The Guilty*: https://www.imdb.com/title/tt6742252/reviews?sort=totalVotes&dir=desc&ratingFilter=0, consulted 14 August 2019.

9   On lateral ellipses, see Guido Kirsten, 'Die Auslassung als Wirklichkeitseffekt. Ellipsen und Lateralellipsen im Film' in *Auslassen, Andeuten, Auffüllen. Der Film und die Imagination des Zuschauers*, edited by Julian Hanich and Hans Jürgen Wulff (Munich: Fink, 2012).

10 Hanich, 'Omission', n.p.

11 Michel Chion, *Audiovision: Sound on Screen* (New York: Columbia University Press, 1994), 74.

12 The term 'medial off' is inspired by Shanyang Zhao's term 'medial co-presence', which I have adopted into my tripartite distinction between immediate, mediate and medial co-presence in the cinema. See Julian Hanich, *The Audience Effect: On the Collective Cinema Experience* (Edinburgh: Edinburgh University Press, 2018), 279–80.

13 Michel Chion, *The Voice in Cinema* (New York: Columbia University Press, 1999), 64.

14 Friedrich Knilli, *Das Hörspiel in der Vorstellung der Hörer: Selbstbeobachtungen* (Frankfurt am Main: Peter Lang, 2006), 40–1.

15 Anežka Kuzmičová, 'Audiobooks and Print Narrative: Similarities in Text Experience' in *Audionarratology: Interfaces of Sound and Narrative*, edited by Jarmila Mildorf and Till Kinzel (Berlin: De Gruyter, 2016), 217–37 (224).

16 What I sketch here are idealized readers and listeners: someone driving a car while listening to a radio drama does not have this possibility; and a reader trying to concentrate on a book while sitting in a crowded subway might find it difficult to imagine the narrative world.

17 Kuzmičová, 'Audiobooks and Print Narrative', 221.

18 Rossana De Beni and Angelica Moeè, 'Presentation Modality Effects in Studying Passages: Are Mental Images Always Effective?', *Applied Cognitive Psychology* 17:3 (2003), 309–24 (311).

19 At some point in *Krapp's Last Tape* the eponymous character even hugs the tape recorder he listens to and lays his head on it, as if to focus even more intensely.

20 Rachel Sherwood and Joel Pearson, 'Closing the Mind's Eye: Incoming Luminance Signals Disrupt Visual Imagery', *PLoS ONE* 5:12 (2010).

21 See Julian Hanich, 'Suggestive Verbalizations in Film: On Character Speech and Sensory Imagination', *New Review of Film and Television Studies* (forthcoming).

22 Emily T. Troscianko, 'Reading Imaginatively: The Imagination in Cognitive Science and Cognitive Literary Studies', *Journal of Literary Semantics* 42:2 (2013), 181–98 (188). See also Anežka Kuzmičová, *Mental Imagery in the Experience of Literary Narrative: Views from Embodied Cognition* (Dissertation. Stockholm University, 2013), 74.

23 Thor Grünbaum, 'Action between Plot and Discourse', *Semiotica* 165:1/4 (2007), 295–314.

24 Anežka Kuzmičová, 'Presence in the Reading of Literary Narrative: A Case for Motor Enactment', *Semiotica* 189:1/4 (2012), 23–48 (31).

25 Don Ihde, *Listening and Voice: Phenomenologies of Sound*, 2nd edition (New York: State University of New York Press, 2007), 170.

26 Quoted in Troscianko, 'Reading Imaginatively', 186.

27 Troscianko, 'Reading Imaginatively', 186.

28 On de-acousmatization, see Chion, *Audio-Vision*, 130–1.

29 Rudolf Arnheim: *Radio* (London: Faber & Faber, 1936), 112.

30 Michel Chion, *Sound: An Acoulogical Treatise* (Durham, NC: Duke University Press, 2016), 114.

31 Chion, *Audio-Vision*, 114.

32 Arnheim, *Radio*, 95.

The Auditory Imagination and the Polyphony of Listening: A Study of Chantal Akerman's *South* (1999)

ALBERTINE FOX

A percussive concoction of mechanical sounds, nature sounds, metallic humming and sinister rumbles dominates the sonic experience of Chantal Akerman's *South* (1999). *South* is a documentary shot in Jasper County, Texas, in the aftermath of the racially motivated murder of an African American musician, named James Byrd, Jr., by three white supremacists. The film's editor, Claire Atherton, insists that *South* is not 'about' racism in a thematic sense. It is not about the black community, or the history of slavery, or even the murder itself, but it is predominantly concerned with feelings and with 'the dialectic between the present, the landscapes, this murder and the past'.[1] Struck by the violent silence and heat of the Deep South, Akerman sought to understand how a bloody history can be evoked by and inscribed in the bucolic surroundings. She wanted to express the nauseous 'feeling of horror' arising from 'almost too much happiness', stirred up in Renoirian fashion by an innocent trip to the countryside.[2]

It is important to recognize that the 'silences' in *South* are brimming with sound. The ambient sound functions as a kind of relative silence that highlights the presence of an active listener. Critics of the film tend to ignore the auditory dynamics shaping the dialectic between present and past. Rose Capp describes the film as 'disconcertingly naïve', a film whose 'roll-call of interviewees foregrounds Akerman's allegiances, while failing to illuminate the problems of American racial politics'. She suggests that the horrifying accounts of the murder, along with the footage of the memorial service, 'border on the exploitative', while the repetitive images of the church, the streets and the countryside make Akerman's 'formalist obsessions' resemble a kind of conceit.[3] Jonathan

Paragraph 43.3 (2020): 265–280
DOI: 10.3366/para.2020.0340
© Edinburgh University Press
www.euppublishing.com/para

Rosenbaum's disparaging appraisal compares *South* to 'sympathetic tourism', arguing that Akerman's 'lack of a personal connection to the American South' forces her to 'function mostly as a journalist'. Commenting on the final tracking shot of the road along which Byrd, Jr.'s body, chained to a pick-up truck, was dragged, Rosenbaum concludes that Akerman can only 'bear mute witness to the crime'.[4] However, her wordless act of witnessing does not take place in a vacuum. By discounting the expressive significance of the ambient soundscape that draws attention to the silent but active listening presence of the filmmaker and her crew, Rosenbaum fails to truly listen to the sequence. As the work of psychoanalyst Dori Laub has confirmed, the process of bearing witness to a trauma must include a listener. The whole of *South* can be thought of as a testimonial process that requires 'a bonding, the intimate and total presence of an *other* — in the position of one who hears.'[5]

I will approach the film from an auditory perspective, inspired by Don Ihde's phenomenological exploration of silence and the 'polyphony of experience', an expression he uses to account for the role of the imagination in one's auditory experience of the world. Rather than listening monophonically to sound's perceptual presence, polyphonic listening means attending also to the ways in which we imaginatively hear or remember a sound. In *South*, the active silences, made palpable by the open landscape shots, resemble negative spaces that give material form to a persistent feeling of absence. I will suggest that the aural force of these shots transforms them into transitory listening spaces, whose reverberant presence forbids the erasure of history and denies a comfortable closure on past trauma. The sensory richness and historical weight of these listening spaces weakens the gravitational pull of the interviews themselves, compelling the audience to listen to the layered visions and sounds of buried pasts, connected to disparate sites of racialized violence. Drawing on Max Silverman's concept of palimpsestic memory, I contend that *South* performs 'a politics of memory founded on a poetics of memory'. This is a hybrid conception of memory functioning as a dynamic, critical space that 'opens up the bland surface of the present to the "knotted intersections" of history'.[6] Informed by Paul Gilroy's work on cultural memory and Michael Rothberg's concept of multidirectional memory, palimpsestic memory counters the compartmentalization of memory based on an ethnic essentialism, and it opposes notions of 'competitive memory' and comparative atrocities, by perceiving memories alongside other memories, forming potential 'solidarities across lines of ethno-cultural division'.[7] In my analysis, notions of 'alongside' and 'across' will also be interpreted along sonic lines, in terms of resonance and reverberation. In a broader sense, my study is supported by two conceptions of the imagination that I construe in terms of listening: one is set out by Toni Morrison in her essay 'The Site of Memory' (1987), and the other by Hannah Arendt in 'Understanding and Politics' (1954).

Imagination, Listening and Emotional Memory

Arendt describes her conception of imagination through reference to a biblical source, citing King Solomon's old prayer to God for the gift of an 'understanding heart' ['leb shama']. She equates the power of the imagination to the capacity to 'catch at least a glimpse of the always frightening light of truth'.[8] Yet she disregards the significance of the Hebrew expression 'leb shama', where *shama* means 'to hear, listen to, obey' and *leb* connotes 'the inner man, mind, will, heart, or understanding'.[9] This observation foregrounds the relationship between listening and the ability to make wise ethical judgements. Arendt then elaborates, associating the imagination with the dialogue of understanding:

Imagination alone enables us to see things in their proper perspective, to be strong enough to put that which is too close at a certain distance so that we can see and understand it without bias and prejudice, to be generous enough to bridge abysses of remoteness until we can see and understand everything that is too far away from us as though it were our own affair. This distancing of some things and bridging the abysses to others is part of the dialogue of understanding (. . .).[10]

Akerman's sensitivity to the framing of each shot and the boundaries of silence generates a posture of receptivity, in the production of her cinema of listening, whose most distinctive trait is a need for connection with the other and a need to distance the other.

Just as Arendt associates the imagination with the glimpsing of a truth, Morrison is less concerned with the difference between fact and fiction than she is with fact and truth, remarking that truth relies on human intelligence to exist. At the start of her essay, she positions herself as an African American woman writer. Her literary heritage comprises the autobiography, whose print origins in black literature lie in African American slave narratives. Working against the tradition of erasure that plagued the slave narrative, whereby gruesome details of the writer's traumatic experiences were omitted to avoid offending the white reader, Morrison's task, as a twentieth-century writer, is 'to rip that veil drawn over "proceedings too terrible to relate"'.[11] She comments on Simone de Beauvoir's recounting of her mother's death in *A Very Easy Death* (1964), and on James Baldwin's depiction of his relationship with his father in *Notes of a Native Son* (1955). Distinguishing herself from these authors, who move from 'the event to the image that it left', Morrison moves in reverse: to expose a glimmer of truth pertaining to the interior life of people whose stories remain unwritten, Morrison insists that the image 'comes first and tells me what the "memory" is about'.[12] Her notion of 'image' denotes not a symbol but a '"picture" and the feelings that accompany the picture'. Since she cannot rely solely on her own memories, or on the recollections of others, to access these missing stories, Morrison must turn to the act of imagination. Naming her approach a form of 'literary archaeology', she explains: '[o]n the basis of some information and a little bit of guesswork you journey to a site to see what remains were left behind and to reconstruct the world that these remains imply'.[13] The atmosphere of emotion surrounding the 'picture' that Morrison describes, echoes Arendt's association of the imagination with the 'peculiar density' surrounding all that is real.[14]

For Morrison, imagination is entangled with memory and she uses the metaphor of the Mississippi River, when it floods the surrounding region, to convey the act of remembering in terms of a rush of imagination. The water breaks its banks because it is remembering where it was before the river was 'straightened out' to allow for the building of new homes. She compares the memory of water to that of writers, who, as sentient beings, attempt to remember the sensory details of where they were, including 'what valley we ran through, what the banks were like, the light that was there and the route back to our original place'. Morrison clarifies that as a black woman writer, to 'extend, fill in and complement' slave narratives, or to reconstruct a world inhabited by people who have been excluded from the discourse purporting to be 'about' them, she must also engage the imagination.

The displacement involved in the writer's act of remembering recalls Akerman's journeying from East Germany to Moscow during the making of *D'Est* (1993) that unlocked an unknown site of trauma — the self-proclaimed 'primal scene' of her oeuvre — connected to her mother's non-narrated traumatic past.[15] Morrison's understanding of imaginative recollection resonates with Akerman's desire to fill in the blanks of her own story ('a story full of holes' due to the absence of family memories) with imaginary memories.[16] The process of remembering as a kind of 'flooding' that is bound to the imagination is described by Morrison as 'emotional memory — what the nerves and the skin remember as well as how it appeared'.[17] Merging the singular with the collective, the process of emotional memory, which surges forth arbitrarily and uncontrollably, permits deep emotions and sensations, buried in the historical unconscious, to surface.

Comparable to Morrison's practice of literary excavation, Akerman journeys to a site, at once familiar and unfamiliar, and creatively reconstructs a world. She does so by imaginatively grasping the feeling-states arising from her sensory experience of place, which is charged with the affective content of the stories she hears and with her own imagined memories connected to the traces left by the historical trauma of the Holocaust. As I will demonstrate, through the relational encounters she stages with the sonorous 'face' of the landscape, Akerman cinematically renders something of the interior life of Jasper and its people, but only by accessing the blanks of her own interior life, as part of the hybrid poetics of memory that lies at the heart of *South*.

The final shot of the film allegorizes this process of imaginative recollection by taking us on a literal journey down the road where the victim's body was so brutally dragged. The prior interview with a local resident named John Craig, who conveys the horror of Byrd, Jr.'s murder by noting where his body was progressively dismembered, generates disturbing images in the spectator's mind that heighten the intensity of the disorienting emotion felt during the ghostly re-enactment that follows. The tracking shot polyphonically fuses imaginative and perceptual modes of experience, a process that depends on an ability to listen to the active silences and see beyond the immediately visible. The camera aligns the spectator with the sensorial position of the killers, who would have felt corporeally, but from the safe distance of their vehicle, the bumps in the road, the vibrations of the engine and the rumbling soundscape. Refusing to turn away from abhorrent brutality, Akerman places herself alongside the spectator in a non-neutral position, as they look back at the road from the raised vantage point of the truck, coming face to face with a disturbing complicity, whose irresolution ensures its endurance in the spectator's mind.

From Monophonic to Polyphonic Listening

From the opening credits of the film, the sound of nature's (artificial)
paradise lulls us into a false sense of security. We sense that the
peacefulness is hiding something sinister. Could the buzzing sound
signal flies and the presence of a rotting corpse? By giving prominence
to the ambient sound design from the start, Akerman cultivates a sort
of hyperrealist silence, tasked with teaching us how to listen to its
fullness. As Laub instructs in his essay on listening to trauma, this
skilled activity demands that we 'recognize, acknowledge and address
that silence, even if this simply means respect — and knowing how to
wait'.[18] Ihde describes listening and waiting as a '"letting be" which
allows that which continuously "is given" into space and time to be
noted', and this process of waiting constitutes a 'listening to silence
which surrounds sound'.[19]

When Akerman searches for the right distance from which to film,
she is not only concerned with the visual parameters of the shot but
with the silences that infuse each image and surround each instance
of speech. Ihde suggests that silence can be understood as a visual
category because it is given in absence. It belongs to 'mute objects'
such as a vase, a pen or a tree, and to 'the syncopation of experiences
in which what is seen seems silent while what is not seen may sound'.[20]
In *South*, this mute presence constitutes a relative silence that resides in
the gaps between the interview scenes, namely, in the discomforting
tranquillity of the landscape shots. The film's intensification of the
ambient soundscape shifts our attention to the hidden side of the visible
image. Ihde writes: '[w]hen I view a thing it presents itself to me
with *a face*. A deeper and more careful analysis reveals that it is not
just *a surface* face, but a face that is an appearance that presents itself
as "having a back" as well.'[21] Significantly, *South* begins not with a
human face but with a mix of sounds that signal an active silence. The
first shot is composed of a Baptist church and a field, accompanied
by the diegetic sound of a man cutting grass. This locatable sound is
unsettled by disorienting rumbles. I hear the blocks of background
sound that permeate *South* as interstices or syncopations that resemble
negative spaces in sculptural art works. As the film progresses, they
enable Akerman to denaturalize the verbal authority of the interviews,
freeing her to address the silent 'back' of the face-to-face encounter,
which is also a listening encounter, displacing the focus from individual
memories to collective histories. These histories require the audience

to participate in a process of listening as a form of witnessing, but a listening attuned to sensory qualities as much as to the narrational act.

The first tracking shot takes place along a street, showing the fronts of people's houses. The curved sides of the frame indicate the presence of the filmmaker who we presume is positioned inside a car looking out through the window. These dark corners at the edges of the screen return throughout the film and highlight the impure, mediated nature of the spectacle, reminding us of Akerman's presence as a listener, an interviewer and a witness. Yet they also carry connotations of the disciplinary regime of surveillance, marking Akerman's self-critical awareness of her role as a controlling 'overseer'. Nevertheless, following Laub, her primary posture is that of an empathetic listener, whose duty throughout the testimonial process is 'to be *unobtrusively present*'.[22] A man drives past in his white truck, and he waves at the camera and utters some words, perhaps thanking the crew for giving way, staging an initial encounter between the receptivity of the spectating subject and the communicative presence of the other. As the engine sounds soften, the spectator is adequately primed to listen, alongside the filmmaker, to the first interview that ensues with a woman named Cora Jones.

This is where Ihde's concept of the polyphony of experience can offer a fresh perspective on the interview scenes that appear on first glance as isolated talking-head shots, contained and reified by the camera. Positioned in a rocking chair on her porch and surrounded by her children, when Cora begins to speak we listen to her voice monophonically, as the receiver of its sound, while tuning in cerebrally to the content of her words. Gradually, though, the audience becomes aware of the 'second modality of experience' outlined by Ihde, consisting of the co-presence of imagination.[23] We notice the wooden lattice behind Cora that kindles the prison metaphor haunting the *mise en scène* in many of Akerman's films and is redolent of her mother's harrowing experiences in the death camps.[24] We also notice the silent presence of Cora's children, who communicate through the hidden language of their inner thoughts, hinted at via their facial expressions and fidgety movements. At the same time, we become aware of the fragility of Cora's speech. This occurs when we hear a car passing, the muffled squeak of its horn and remnants of the buzzing nature sounds. These sonic details remind us of the dubiously anodyne soundscape from the film's opening that could at any moment rush in and overwhelm Cora's words.

Our auditory memory of these earlier sounds doubles the perceived sound of Cora's audible speech, shifting our listening from the monophonic to the polyphonic mode. The accumulation of marginal sonic and kinetic details causes the scene to stammer and reminds us that the interviewee's speech is part of an ideologically constructed soundtrack. For example, the fidgety rustlings form a line of solidarity with the gentle diegetic clicking sound from a prior shot of a woman sitting alone on her porch, preparing the edible parts of a vegetable. This precise sound of an everyday chore that has a clear directional location is cushioned by an ambiguous metallic whirring. This sonic blend then evolves into the clinking of a KCS tanker train that is seen rattling past in the next shot, as if to implicitly reference Holocaust journeys to the camps. The rattling sound mutates into the engine sounds accompanying the aforementioned tracking shot, which ricochets with the film's final shot of the deserted road, raising questions of complicity with the white supremacist killers. Akerman's soundtrack becomes meaningful in an accumulative manner as she crafts an aural archive from the sounds of everyday life, blemished by audiovisual memories of unconscionable horror. The interview with Cora, then, is not as isolated as it might appear because it forms part of a wider testimonial process of listening that blurs the lines between the individual and the collective, and between perpetrator, spectator and victim, producing a hybrid critical space activated by the imaginative act.

A long shot follows the interview, expanding our perceptual field from the personal to the communal. Our auditory focus is also enlarged as we engage in a 'field state' mode of listening that according to Ihde corresponds to 'the visual taking in of an entire vista'.[25] We see members of the congregation leaving the church, possibly exiting the memorial service of Byrd, Jr., that features later. This outdoor shot is accompanied by the rousing sound of singing emanating from the interior. The lengthy duration of this shot that constitutes the aftermath of Cora's narration, offers an interlude for reflection. This listening space allows the palimpsestic interconnections to surface between the singular, racist hate crime and the wider history recounted by Cora, who speaks of racial segregation and the enslavement of African Americans before the Civil Rights Movement of the 1960s. The long take enables us to listen to the active silence of an auditory imaginative *presencing* of Cora's now absent voice that resounds in our mind.

The acousmatic sound of singing involves us in an aural scene of community, as the excesses of the auditory imagination mobilize the prior interview whose presence loiters on. The spectator's imagined auditory appearance of Cora mingles with the audible chorus of the bereaved, producing a polyphony of experience that combines the perceptual with the imaginative, and the present with the immediate past. Atherton explains how the images surrounding Cora's interview do not *illustrate* her words, for, she is 'in resonance with' the other images.[26] The informative power of her speech is not permitted to dominate, but it exists as one element alongside the other images and sounds that make contact with each other owing to the binding temporal flow of reverberation.

South's reverberant aesthetic of 'alongside' engenders the 'politics of sides' that Sara Ahmed describes in her discussion of Countee Cullen's poem 'Tableau', cited by So Mayer in their captivating study of *South*. Ahmed writes: 'one is not asked to "take sides" when one is "beside" — one walks beside and alongside.'[27] This 'radicalization of the side', which can be discerned in the poem's reference to a black boy and a white boy walking together in unison, whose proximity, Ahmed argues, produces a queer effect, is intensified in *South* through its privileging of what I have called the 'back' of the interview, which echoes Ahmed's construal of 'the inverted face'. She writes that for Merleau-Ponty, whose description of the face as an 'oriented' object gains its significance from its orientation, then if the face was inverted, becoming 'queer', by no longer facing 'the right way', it would be deprived of its significance. For Ahmed, this is the moment when the face 'slips away' to become distant and oblique to what coheres along privileged heteronormative lines, which are racially regulated so as to remain free from racial impurity, invisibly coded as white. Ahmed suggests that a queer orientation might involve seeing the inverted face not as marred by a loss of significance, but that through its 'retreat', a path is cleared for 'new shapes and directions' to emerge.[28]

Whereas Mayer proposes that *South* fails to become a surface for proximity 'between those who are supposed to live on parallel lines, *as points that should not meet*', referencing Ahmed's discussion of the queer disorientation of the black body, I want to suggest that the listening spaces in *South* accent the moment when the interview 'slips', creating the possibility for 'new lines to gather as expressions that we do not yet know how to read'.[29] The breathing space given to the auditory imagination provides an unseen surface for contact that requires one to listen backwards, forwards and diagonally across the film.

During the shot described above, following Cora's interview, we see a girl, dressed in a bright yellow dress, leaving the church. She walks towards the camera, positioned between several rows of black and white parked cars. The vibrancy of her dress and the positioning of her body offer hope that, by claiming the space 'in between' the cars, the essentializing binary of black versus white could be undone. This dream is short-lived as she trails off to the side, leaving the dichotomy in place. However, the girl soon reappears, returning to the centre of the shot, swinging her arms and glancing back knowingly at the camera. Then a young man exits the church and walks the path she forged, striding between the cars, followed by a little boy, as if to secure a new route for the next generation. Finally, the girl returns and begins to walk again towards the camera, now joined by another girl, who is wearing a similar yellow dress, and an older woman dressed in pink (see Figure 1). They pass triumphantly together, as an all-female unit, through the space 'in-between'. This sequence functions only on a symbolic level, but it constitutes an example of what Mayer shrewdly identifies as a 'minor model of solidarity and collaboration' that also 'suggests a queer possibility' by gesturing towards a future of greater cross-racial union.[30]

The duration of this shot permits the stammering of Cora's interview to join forces with the sensorial power of yellow. This layering of sound, speech and colour forms an imaginary parental bond between Cora and the girl, perhaps suggestive of Akerman's personal desire for greater connection with her mother. The shot of the girls walking together between the cars simultaneously hints at a queer moment, owing to the sensory excess produced by the bright colours, enhanced by the spectator's imaginative recollection of the chorus of voices that resounded moments earlier. Calling to mind other disorienting moments of domestic disorder and sensory disruption in Akerman's films, this confluence of sensation allows Cora, the girl and her female companions to temporarily transcend the constraints of the frame.

Listening beyond a Lenticular Logic

While neither Capp nor Rosenbaum listen closely to the sonic construction of *South*, the crux of each critic's argument is important

Figures 1 and 2. *South* (Chantal Akerman, 1999).

to consider. They point to the lack of any sustained attempt, on Akerman's part, to turn her critical gaze on the racial construction of whiteness. The disembodied status of the filmmaker and crew can be deemed problematic in that it adds fuel to the dangerous notion of whiteness as an unmarked, invisible norm, against which the racialized other is defined. In Morrison's *Playing in the Dark*, this danger is encapsulated by her analogy of the fishbowl: she sees the fish moving, surrounded by traces of foliage, food and bubbles. Then suddenly she notices the bowl itself, 'the structure that transparently (and invisibly) permits the ordered life it contains to exist in the larger world'.[31] The bowl represents the concealed ideology of whiteness that surrounds the fish, controlling how race is represented in the American literary imagination. Citing bell hooks's critique of *Paris is Burning* (Livingston 1990), Mayer takes up this line of thought, suggesting that Akerman fails to show clearly enough 'WHO made this picture'. For Mayer, Akerman's absence from the frame 'could be said, at its extremes, to assume "an imperial overseeing position that is in no way progressive or counterhegemonic"'.[32] Akerman can certainly be criticized for not engaging more overtly with the interracial harmony that exists in Jasper, and for not proactively highlighting the town's history of activist struggles that made cross-racial alliance possible. The lack of scrutiny given to the South's expanding population and its economic and technological advances misleadingly accentuates the reverse picture of poverty and negativity, as Marie Liénard warns in her analysis of the film.[33] However, the neglected role of the soundtrack and the hybrid conception of memory that *South* enacts means that it cannot be so easily dismissed for presenting a static vision of race, anchored in the black/white axis that supports the binary logic central to white supremacy.

South's hyperbolic display of black versus white intentionally throws light on the visual codes of race by performatively staging the 'monocular' logic of racial visibility that Tara McPherson terms a 'lenticular logic'. A lenticular image consists of the combining of two distinct images but when viewed through a lenticular lens, one can only see one of the two images at a time. This logic refuses copresence and allows 'whiteness to float free from blackness', denying 'productive overlap or connection, forestalling doubled vision and precluding alliance'.[34] The visual patterning of black and white cars, black and white tankers, images of white birds perched next to water, followed by a shot of a brown calf swimming, are uncomfortably marked by the separatist logic of the lenticular. As Liénard notes, these images are fleetingly offset by an image of a brown puppy and a blond puppy, filmed within the same frame, playing together in the grass, thus raising the possibility of coexistence.[35] Significantly, the listener is not confined to such a rigid and superficial epidermal logic, and it is the soundtrack that lifts the film out of a regressive, binary simulation of racial difference. By teaching the spectator to listen to the relative silences, Akerman punctuates the superimpositions and reverberations that can be linked to the non-lenticular power of doubled vision, whose aural counterpart is polyphonic listening, which requires an attentiveness to the copresence of perceptual *and* imaginative modes of experience.

One of the interviewees, Dereck Mohammed, states that the goal of white supremacists is to restore white pride to Jasper by eradicating the presence of black people. He refers to the period of anxiety following Emancipation, when white masculine supremacists feared African American men becoming 'real men'. Here he is alluding to the ingrained association of the black male with the phallic lack of the feminine, as Robyn Wiegman underlines in her study of the practice of lynching in the United States. She states that this association had been brutally materialized 'through the frequent accompaniment of castration and lynching', a legacy referenced in *South* during the interviews with Mrs Callins and Jonathan Callins.[36]

Akerman cites Baldwin's evocation of lynching trees as a key influence on *South*. In 'Nobody Knows My Name: A Letter from the South', Baldwin describes his first impressions of the 'rust-red earth' of Georgia, as his plane hovered over the treetops before landing: 'I could not suppress the thought that this earth had acquired its colour from the blood that had dripped down from these trees. My mind was filled with the image of a black man, younger than I, perhaps, or my own age, hanging from a tree, while white men watched him and cut his sex from him with a knife.'[37] Three open landscape shots of trees follow Dereck's interview: the first and third feature a reappearance of the dark curves framing the shot, reminding us of Akerman's close listening presence. The second shows a barbed-wire fence in front of a field. This lengthy shot is accompanied by the rustling of crickets and the sound of a helicopter, suggesting punitive regimes of surveillance. The rumblings of a train and the increasing volume of ambient sound attunes our attention to the inhuman hum of cinema's own act of remembering. Indeed, this shot recalls the opening images, filmed at Auschwitz, of barbed wire, grass and trees in Alain Resnais's *Night and Fog* (1955), accompanied by Jean Cayrol's voiceover alluding to the landscape's apparent tranquillity.

Akerman's reimagining of the Deep South does not present a neatly contained world that bears no relation to the world outside the curved 'bowl' of its frame. *South* spills over the edges of its geographic location and engenders a form of 'concentrationary memory' that Silverman distinguishes from 'Holocaust memory' through its denial of specificity, evading 'any such ethno-cultural or religious particularization'. It shows us 'how the particular is always haunted by its absent other', thereby contaminating the lenticular logic with a spectral copresence.[38] The spindly metallic sound accompanying the third landscape shot is almost violent. It charges the mute object of the silvery tree — the inverted face — that faces us, with the absent depth of its 'other side', namely, the sound of silence (see Figure 2). This silence constitutes the ghostly memory of an act of lynching, doubled by the echoes of the death camps from the previous shot. The shot of the tree is ever so slightly tainted by the curve at the bottom left-hand corner of the screen.

To an extent, these recurrent window shots, indicating the director's listening presence, articulate an acknowledgement of the privileged context of whiteness within which she is operating. Yet it is vital to recognize that they also point up an awareness of the racial ambivalence of her Jewishness, as a queer Jewish woman, and this acknowledgement cannot be separated from her status as a white francophone filmmaker. *South* performs moments of contact across history that sees Akerman's subjective questioning of racist ideology and racialized violence, put anti-black racism and white supremacy into dialogue with evocations of Jewish oppression, through her staging of concentrationary memory.

As she crafts a cinematic archaeology of her own, Akerman listens with and beyond the facts of the crime and the content of the testimonies, tracing, via the distancing and proximity of her camera, the 'emotional memory' of shared human suffering. The multidirectional nature of her engagement with memory and trauma cannot be deemed merely journalistic. Neither can it be understood in a 'them/us' imperialistic vein, serving an individualistic journey of self-discovery, dependent on the insights offered by the 'other', whose presence is erased in the process. Not seeking to compare atrocities, *South* creates 'negative' listening spaces conducive to a contrapuntal idea of memory as an imaginative act, that gives form to the 'non-forms' of hidden voices, stories and histories. In exploiting the full silence of ambient sound, *South* compels the audience to confront their role as active listeners absorbed in the polyphony of experience. By listening polyphonically to the film, weaving perceptual and imaginative experience into a complex form of copresence, the spectator participates in the cinematic process of imaginative recollection and reconstruction. The protean nature of this process prevents the congealing of an *unfelt*, monologic interpretation that turns away from the vivid presentness of the past.

NOTES

1   Tina Poglajen, 'Interview: Claire Atherton', *Film Comment*, 2 November 2016, https://www.filmcomment.com/blog/interview-claire-atherton/, consulted 1 July 2019.

2   Marion Schmid, *Chantal Akerman* (Manchester: Manchester University Press, 2010), 111.

3   Rose Capp, 'Akerman Resists Southern Comfort', *Senses of Cinema*, 6 (May 2000), http://sensesofcinema.com/2000/feature-articles/south/, consulted 15 July 2019.

4   Jonathan Rosenbaum, 'Place and Displacement: Akerman and Documentary', *Jonathan Rosenbaum*, 29 March 2016, http://www.jonathanrosenbaum. net/2016/03/place-and-displacement-akerman-and-documentary/, consulted 1 February 2019.

5   Dori Laub, M.D., 'Bearing Witness, or the Vicissitudes of Listening' in Shoshana Felman and Dori Laub, M.D., *Testimony: Crises of Witnessing in Literature, Psychoanalysis, and History* (New York: Routledge, 1992), 57–74 (70), original emphasis.

6   Max Silverman, *Palimpsestic Memory: The Holocaust and Colonialism in French and Francophone Fiction and Film* (New York: Berghahn Books, 2013), 8 and 22.

7   Silverman, *Palimpsestic Memory*, 20–1.

8   Hannah Arendt, 'Understanding and Politics (The Difficulties of Understanding)' in *Essays in Understanding 1930–1954: Formation, Exile, and Totalitarianism*, edited by Jerome Kohn (New York: Schocken Books, 1994), 307–32 (322).

9   Richard Blackaby (ed.), *Blackaby Study Bible: Personal Encounters with God through His Word* (Nashville, TN: Thomas Nelson, 2006), 400.

10 Arendt, 'Understanding and Politics', 323.

11 Morrison, 'The Site of Memory', 237–38.

12 Morrison, 'The Site of Memory', 239–40.

13 Morrison, 'The Site of Memory', 238.

14 Arendt, 'Understanding and Politics', 322.

15 Griselda Pollock, *After-affects/After-images: Trauma and Aesthetic Transformation in the Virtual Feminist Museum* (Manchester: Manchester University Press, 2013), 328.

16 Janet Bergstrom suggests that most of Akerman's films are motivated by the need to *create* memories in order 'to mourn and to make up for the disruption of a continuous oral tradition passed down from one generation to the next, most importantly from mother to daughter'. See Bergstrom, 'Invented Memories' in *Identity and Memory: The Films of Chantal Akerman*, edited by Gwendolyn Audrey Foster (Trowbridge: Flicks Books, 1999), 94–116 (98).

17 Morrison, 'The Site of Memory', 243.

18 Laub, 'Bearing Witness', 58.

19   Don Ihde, *Listening and Voice: Phenomenologies of Sound*, 2nd edition (Albany: State University of New York Press, 2007), 109–11.

20   Ihde, *Listening and Voice*, 110.

21   Ihde, *Listening and Voice*, 110.

22   Laub, 'Bearing Witness', 71.

23   Ihde, *Listening and Voice*, 117.

24   Marion Schmid, 'The Cinema Films Back: Colonialism, Alterity and Resistance in Chantal Akerman's *La Folie Almayer*', *Australian Journal of French Studies* 51:1 (2014), 22–34 (27).

25   Ihde, *Listening and Voice*, 102.

26   Claire Atherton, 'The Art of Editing', Masterclass from the Tel-Aviv International Student Film Festival, 11 June 2016, https://www.youtube.com/watch?v=uW8yuCkwjZw, consulted 10 April 2019 [31:30].

27   Sara Ahmed, *Queer Phenomenology: Orientations, Objects, Others* (Durham, NC: Duke University Press, 2006), 169.

28   Ahmed, *Queer Phenomenology*, 171–2.

29   So Mayer, 'Texas (is Not Paris) is Burning: The Drag of Dis/Orientation in Chantal Akerman's *Sud*' in *Chantal Akerman: Afterlives*, edited by Marion Schmid and Emma Wilson (Oxford: Legenda, 2019), 102–14 (106); Ahmed, *Queer Phenomenology*, 171.

30   Mayer, 'Texas (is Not Paris) is Burning', 108. I am indebted to Emma Wilson and attendees of the Cambridge Film and Screen Studies research seminar (October 2018) for their invaluable feedback on my initial analysis of this sequence.

31   Toni Morrison, *Playing in the Dark: Whiteness and the Literary Imagination* (Cambridge, MA: Harvard University Press, 1992), 17.

32   Mayer, 'Texas (is Not Paris) is Burning', 109–13.

33   Marie Liénard, '*Sud* de Chantal Akerman ou une histoire de territoire et de terre: le Sud comme espace de mémoire', *Caliban: French Journal of English Studies* 19 (2006), 131–8 (para. 26), https://journals.openedition.org/caliban/2416#bodyftn10.

34   Tara McPherson, *Reconstructing Dixie: Race, Gender, and Nostalgia in the Imagined South* (Durham, NC: Duke University Press, 2003), 7 and 27.

35   Liénard, '*Sud* de Chantal Akerman', para. 25.

36   Robyn Wiegman, *American Anatomies: Theorizing Race and Gender* (Durham, NC: Duke University Press, 1995), 14.

37   James Baldwin, *Nobody Knows My Name: More Notes of a Native Son* (London: Penguin Books, 1991), 88; Chantal Akerman, *Chantal Akerman: Autoportrait en cinéaste* (Paris: Éditions du Centre Pompidou/Cahiers du cinéma, 2004), 233.

38   Silverman, *Palimpsestic Memory*, 48.

Imagining Cinema: 'Cinempathy' and the Embodied Imagination

ROBERT SINNERBRINK

One of the most dynamic topics in philosophical film theory is the role of emotion in our engagement with cinematic works.[1] From being relatively neglected, emotional engagement, in particular the role of empathy/sympathy in narrative fiction,[2] has attracted renewed attention from theorists drawing on a wide range of perspectives (phenomenological approaches, cognitivist theories, philosophical aesthetics, to neuroscientific and evolutionary studies).[3] Theorists of emotional engagement, especially those concerned with empathy/sympathy, have increasingly turned to *imagination* to explain how we engage with fiction, respond emotionally to characters, and arrive at moral evaluations of what we experience on screen.[4] Imagination, moreover, has become a major topic in contemporary aesthetics.[5] Theorists have investigated its perceptual, emotional, cognitive and aesthetic dimensions, as well as its relationship with memory, belief and desire. Although it plays an essential role in linking hypothetical thinking and emotional engagement with aesthetic and ethical experience, the imagination itself has received comparatively little attention in film theory and film-philosophy.

In what follows, I examine these related topics of inquiry — emotional engagement, empathy/sympathy and (moral) imagination in cinema — and argue that imagination plays an essential role in linking emotional engagement with moral-ethical experience in response to cinematic works. To this end, I consider competing accounts of imagination (drawing on phenomenological, cognitive, psychological and aesthetic perspectives), focusing on the idea of *perceptual* imagining, and suggest that an account of *embodied cinematic imagination* encompassing both perceptual/sensory and propositional/cognitive imagining — is especially relevant to

Paragraph 43.3 (2020): 281–297
DOI: 10.3366/para.2020.0341
© Edinburgh University Press
www.euppublishing.com/para

theorizing cinematic experience. The interplay of first-person empathic and third-person sympathetic perspectives ('cinempathy') is also examined as essential to emotional and ethical engagement with cinema. By synthesizing 'bottom-up' sensory, affective responses to audiovisual images, with 'top-down' cognitive processes associated with mental simulation, an account of embodied cinematic imagination can help explain how emotional engagement and ethical responsiveness work together in our experience of audiovisual narratives.

What is Imagination?

The first challenge facing the theorist of cinematic imagination is to find an appropriate definition of the phenomenon in question. Within the history of aesthetics, imagination has played a central role in mediating between perception and reflection, fantasy and reality, self and other. As Shen-yi Liao and Tamar Gendler observe, however, attempts at taxonomizing imagination have not been very successful. This is due in part to the protean character of the imagination — covering both acts and products — but also because of the disparate phenomena commonly brought together under this category. Leslie Stevenson, for example, explores 'Twelve Conceptions of Imagination', which range from 'the ability to think of something not presently perceived, but spatio-temporally real' to 'the ability to create works of art that express something deep about the meaning of life'.[6] Many theorists, moreover, have been at pains to distinguish psychological or cognitive aspects of imagination from the creative sense of imagination, even though these are clearly linked (in our experience of art, for example, or in practices of artistic creativity).

A glance at the history of aesthetics confirms this view. Kant identified the faculty of imagination as the power of presenting an object in intuition that is not present to our senses; he further divided this capacity into the *productive* imagination (presenting an object that is independent of experience) and the *reproductive* imagination (presenting an object that one has experienced previously). In his text *The Imaginary* (1940), Jean-Paul Sartre argued on phenomenological grounds that imagination is distinct from perception; we can either perceive things or imagine them but not both at once. Images, moreover, are forms of intentional consciousness directed at the world, albeit as objects that have been 'de-realized' and thereby posited as 'present-absent' (the presentation of something absent).[7] For Sartre, the material aspect of an image (the 'analogon', or analogical representation) serves as a visual prop for imagination, which is distinguished from the imaginary element intended by this representation.

The common thread in these conceptions of imagination is the idea of representing an object that is not present to the perceiver, or that does not exist in a form available to present perception. Moreover, although imagination is clearly related to image-formation, it can refer to other sense modalities (for example, aural imaginings and kinaesthetic imaginings). Imagination, moreover, particularly in fiction, also involves entertaining the thought or idea of something without a corresponding belief in it (for example, imagining a character in a fiction without a corresponding belief in its extra-diegetic existence or reality). Imagination is neither the same as perception or as belief, although it entertains complex relations with both; nor is it the same as memory, although both involve what philosophers call 'mental time travel'. At this point we enter upon the vast field of varieties of imagination, from visual imaginings, perceptual imaginings, the phenomenon of 'mental images', cognitive imaginings (like philosophical thought experiments), creative problem solving, visualization techniques, to the phenomenon of artistic originality in creating works of art and the metaphorical sense of imagination as describing a particular mindset or capacity for imagining alternative possibilities.

Fascinating as these different senses of imagination might be, I shall take as primary the idea of imagination as the faculty of representing or rendering an absent object as present, and of entertaining its representation without being committed to various beliefs regarding its referent (like imagining a fictional character or world). I also restrict myself here to the role of imagination in relation to *cinematic experience*, which includes both perceptual imagining and the idea of central or empathic imagination (although propositional and cognitive imagining also play a role). This is an important way of understanding and responding to what Rafe McGregor has called the 'problem of cinematic imagination':[8] namely whether our engagement with cinematic images involves a diminished degree of imaginative engagement (compared with literature, for example), and hence is artistically inferior to other artforms. Following McGregor's response to this problem — namely that cinematic engagement involves a *different*, rather than inferior, kind of imaginative engagement (perceptual and fictional imagining rather than propositional and 'creative' imagining) — I suggest that what we require is an account of *cinematic imagination* that pays due regard to the embodied (sensuous, affective, perceptual and 'bodily') character of this kind of imagining. This will enable us to not only defend the imaginative and aesthetic potentials of cinema but to understand better the relationship between empathy, emotional engagement and cinematic (moral-ethical) imagination.

Cinematic Imagination, Point of View and Empathic Engagement

So what role does imagination play in our emotional engagement with audiovisual narratives? Moreover, how does imaginative involvement relate to ethical evaluation, the phenomenon of 'moral allegiance' and its shaping of normative attitudes? To respond, let us begin with a debate concerning the nature of cinematic representation, the question of what we are seeing when we encounter a point of view (POV) shot. The very name suggests a perspectival view or visual perspective attributable to an observer, sometimes described as 'the camera' (even though the camera, strictly speaking, does not exist within the diegetic world of the film) but more typically understood as a character perspective. Greg Currie has dubbed this view, of which he is critical, the 'imagined observer hypothesis' or as 'psychologism': namely the assumption that shots, particularly POV shots, are attributable to some perceiving observer, whether construed as the viewer somehow 'observing' what occurs within the diegetic world of the film, or else attributable to a character within this world whose perspective the spectator is solicited to adopt.

This view has been sharply criticized, from a variety of perspectives. Currie's cognitivist critique of the 'implied observer hypothesis' argues that it generates perceptual and narrative absurdities (in one of the more remarkable sequences in Alfonso Cuarón's *Gravity* (2013), for example, it would mean I somehow occupy Dr Ryan Stone's (Sandra Bullock's) spacesuit and helmet so as to 'observe' her panicked response as she is cast adrift through space). Deleuzian critics argue that such a position assumes camera shots are assimilable to an anthropocentric perspective centred on the 'natural perception' of a self-conscious subject.[9] Cinema, however, cannot be equated with 'natural perception' and is sometimes described as offering 'non-human' perspectives on the world (what such non-natural, non-human perception looks like, however, is left rather obscure). Nonetheless, it is clear that there are difficulties in ascribing shots, and particularly POV shots, to implied observers, even though there are attempts to defend this view. One response is to suggest that not all implications of such a viewpoint need be accounted for in narrative terms; or that such observers could well be impersonal visual points of view without being attributable to a 'subject' (the camera); or that there are unusual cases where it is narratively meaningful to ascribe a subjective shot to a particular character as revealing their (perceptual) point of view (for example, the famous dolly-zoom shot from Scottie's perspective in Alfred Hitchcock's *Vertigo* (1958)). Or that such questions are simply irrelevant to, or even violate, the rules of the game defining narrative engagement.

One way that POV shots can be understood is via the notion of cinematic imagining. Murray Smith's discussion of central imagining, or 'imagining from the inside', and acentral imagining, or 'imagining from the outside', still offers one of the more productive accounts of imagination in cinema, linking it closely to emotional engagement and cinematic empathy.[10] *Central* imagining involves imagining seeing from a character's perspective (Scottie's experience of vertigo as he hangs from the roof and sees the ground falling away beneath him) whereas *acentral* imagining involves imagining seeing from a viewpoint outside of a character, an impersonal viewpoint *of* a character but not from their point of view (the counter-shot of Scottie gazing down in panicked terror at the ground far below). These concepts correspond to Greg Currie's distinction between *personal* and *impersonal* imagining, that is, imagining seeing from 'one's own' perspective within the fictional world versus imagining seeing from a perspective not attributable to any subject or agent within that fictional world.[11] As Smith notes, both Currie and Richard Wollheim (from whom these terms are borrowed) take imagining to mean *mental simulation*: 'to imagine is to simulate having beliefs, attitudes, emotions, etc. other than those one really possesses, running our mental processes (as Currie puts it) '"off-line"', that is, 'disconnected from their normal sensory inputs and behavioural outputs'.[12]

Imagining from the inside or central imagining also clearly suggests the phenomenon of *empathy*, or feeling *with* a character, sharing their point of view. We can contrast this with feeling *for* a character, or feeling *sympathy* regarding their plight, imagining from the outside or acentrally what they must be experiencing, which need not imply that one shares their point of view or congruent affective state.

Empathy and sympathy are clearly related, and in the case of cinematic imagining, as I argue below, they are dynamically interrelated as complementary forms of perspective-taking (what I call 'cinempathy'). It is important to note in the case of empathy or central imagining, however, that this need not imply any kind of implausible 'fusion' with the character's perspective or assimilation of all of their relevant attitudes, traits or responses. Rather, one can share a character's perspective, imagining centrally from their point of view, feeling *with* them as to what their experience involves, while nonetheless distinguishing oneself from that character. Indeed, as Amy Coplan notes, this interplay of perceptual and affective perspective taking, where we retain the distinction between self and other, is the hallmark of empathy proper.[13] She thus rejects the view that empathy implies a 'dissolution' of the self–other boundary as well as the view that empathy can be defined by involuntary forms of affective mimicry or emotional contagion alone (i.e. without higher order cognitive imagining).[14] To paraphrase Kant, empathy without the self–other distinction is empty; affective mimicry without imagination is blind.

It is clear that the processes at play in central imagining with respect to cinematic experience also play an important role in ordinary social experience. As many philosophers have argued, the phenomenon of empathy — involving imaginative engagement or mental simulation of the desires, beliefs, attitudes and responses of others — is essential to intersubjective communication and successful social interaction.[15] So-called 'mindreading' is an imaginative activity involving perceptual, affective-emotional and cognitive understanding of others arrived at via complex forms of motor mirroring and mental simulation.[16] It can give rise to coordinated action responses involving not only imagination but affective mimicry, bodily attunement and cognitive reflection within a shared context of meaning.[17] Without such imaginative empathic involvement, it would be difficult to understand, respond to, and predict the behaviour of others (and vice versa), a difficulty painfully apparent in forms of autism. If imagining from the inside, or 'empathizing' (as Alex Neil and Coplan claim), plays a crucial role in intersubjective understanding and social interaction, then it would indeed be 'bizarre', as Smith remarks, 'if it did not play *some* role in fiction films'.[18]

Smith goes on to explore this role of central imagining but also modifies the framework of emotional engagement ('identification') with cinematic fictions as first outlined in his book *Engaging Characters* (1995). Engaging with cinematic fictions involves both acentral and central imagining, with episodes of central imagining being contextualized or 'assimilated' to the broader acentral imagining constituting the fictional world more generally. Under the category of acentral imagining, Smith outlines his well-known model of character engagement (or 'structure of sympathy') as comprising the three distinct levels of structure: *recognition* (identifying characters as individuals with particular traits); *alignment* (understanding character subjectivity via access to their actions, perceptions, and psychological states); and *allegiance* (evaluation of character actions and traits typically involving moral-ethical valuation but also aesthetic considerations). Together these comprise a 'structure of sympathy' that accounts for a large part of our emotional engagement with characters within narrative film.[19]

This is a well-known part of the story, but it does not cover all of it. Under the category of central imagining (or what we could call processes of empathic imagining) Smith proposes three further *processes*: *emotional simulation* (simulating characters' emotional states by way of central or empathic imagining); *affective mimicry* (involuntary mimicry of characters' affective states thanks to bodily gestures, facial expressions or vocal cues); and *autonomic responses* (reflex reactions to powerful aural or visual cues, e.g. the startle reflex or involuntary bodily movements induced by strong audiovisual stimuli). The separation of emotional simulation from involuntary processes such as affective mimicry and autonomic responses offers an important clarification as to how empathic imagining works (Smith offers this clarification in response to criticisms that these tended to be conflated under the concept of 'central imagining'). Smith thus defines emotional simulation as a species of central imagining, one which focuses on imagining the emotional states of others (and is thus clearly aligned with empathy); this should be distinguished from affective mimicry and autonomic responses, which are not imaginings themselves but can serve as supplementary 'aids or prompts' to such imagining.[20] Certain audiovisual cues (such as sound or music), along with affective mimicry induced by close-ups, for example, can stimulate or enhance the work of emotional simulation, making our central imagining more striking, vivid or intense.

The role of POV shots raises important questions concerning the relationship between central versus acentral (or personal versus impersonal) imagining in cinema — a point on which Currie and Smith disagree. For Currie, imagining in cinema is impersonal perceptual imagining: it is perceptual imagining (we perceive a figure, say a well-known actor, but also imagine a fictional character) but also impersonal or acentral imagining (so not attributable to any perceiving subject within the film world, or not requiring the spectator to assume this perceptual perspective). I can see the look of abject terror on Scottie's face as he hangs from the rooftop but do not imagine myself hanging off the roof alongside him or imagine myself being him as I see the ground appear to fall away beneath me. POV shots, however, would seem to offer an obvious counterexample to the claim that cinematic imagination is invariably impersonal perceptual imagining, and the famous dolly-zoom shot of Scottie's experience of vertigo is a case in point. What is this shot if not an experiential presentation of what Scottie perceives (but also feels) as he has an attack of vertigo? The soundtrack accompanying the shot, we should note, is an intrinsic part of its expressive effect, and suggests not only a perceptual but an affective-emotional dimension to its meaning, which adds further weight to the claim that it presents a case of central or empathic imagining.

Currie's response is that we attribute the meaning of the shot to Scottie, that it expresses what his experience is like, not that one imagines oneself in Scottie's shoes: 'subjective shots function to help us imagine what a character's experience is like, not to imagine ourselves being that character or having that experience'.[21] As Smith points out, however, POV shots typically work in conjunction with reaction shots: the POV shot shows us what the character sees or perceives (and, I would add, what he or she feels), while the reaction shot shows the character's attention, reaction or emotional response to what he or she sees (Scottie's shock and fear). Such sequences are embedded in broader narrative sequences that contextualize the POV/reaction shot relationship and provide further background as to the character's subjective state. What is distinctive about POV shots, of course, is their capacity to reveal visually what a character experiences and thereby align us with their point of view. This experiential perspective prompts us to imagine seeing what the character sees (the ground falling away from beneath one's feet) and can thus be described as a kind of central or empathic imagining. The POV shot works together with reaction shots, including audiovisual cues such as lighting, scaling, sound and music, along with the contextual narrative sequencing of images in order to elicit what Smith calls 'multifaceted alignment' with a character's subjective experience.[22] The POV shot offers a prompt for central or empathic imagining, but it can do so only in context: only in conjunction with reaction shots and related audiovisual elements in a sequence can the POV shot be 'fleshed out' in order to reveal the subjective emotional and cognitive experience of a character in all its complexity.

In some cases, POV shots can be used not only to reveal a character's subjective experience but also the reaction of others. Two very different examples come to mind in this context: one from Jonathan Demme's *Silence of the Lambs* (1991) and one from Pedro Almodóvar's *All about My Mother* (1999). The first is the disturbing POV shot from the perspective of armed serial killer 'Buffalo Bill', hiding in a darkened basement wearing night-vision goggles, stalking terrified FBI agent Clarice Starling who is groping blindly in the dark, frantically pointing her gun in the hope of somehow detecting and shooting the killer. The POV shot, framed by the killer's night-goggle vision (accompanied by the sound of the device being switched on and Clarice's heavy breathing), continues for nearly two minutes, revealing his hand reaching out towards Clarice's face and hair before he cocks his gun and prepares to shoot her. The sequence shows us his visual perspective on her but also Clarice's terrified response. POV shot and reaction shot are fused here, but the focus is on Clarice's terrified but brave response rather than the killer's subjective experience (which remains opaque to us). In this case one occupies the visual perspective of the killer but also inhabits the emotional perspective of Clarice. It is a case of central imagining and acentral imagining at once, which combines visual imagining with emotional imagining but restricts empathic/sympathetic engagement to Clarice — both our feeling *with* her (feeling her fear) and feeling *for* her (sympathizing with her plight) — rather than the killer (whom we dearly wish to see killed).

Another example is from Almodóvar's *All about My Mother*: theatre-aficionado and aspiring writer Esteban (Eloy Azorin), the son of former actress turned nurse Manuela (Cecilia Roth), waits after a show to get an autograph from his favourite actress, Huma Rojo (Marisa Paredes), who has just finished performing the role of Blanche in *A Streetcar Named Desire*. He stands in the pouring rain as his mother approaches but then suddenly runs off after the actress's departing taxi in the hope of securing her autograph. The camera stays with his mother, then shows the boy running after the taxi, followed by the screech of brakes as her son is hit by a car and lands on the windscreen. What follows is an extraordinary POV shot, from the dying son's perspective, falling to the ground as his mother runs towards him, the image slowing the motion down as the soundtrack distorts, emphasizing the rain and Manuela's cry, 'My son, my son!'

The sequence stretches the son's dying moments as he sees and hears (as do we) his mother's raw grief, her wailing and crying, as her son's life slips away. This POV shot, from the perspective of the dying son, shows his mother's devastating reaction, combining again the POV with a reaction shot, the slowed image and distorted soundtrack expressing both the son's ebbing consciousness and his mother's traumatic grief. The scene powerfully conveys the experiential intensity of this tragic event, for both son and mother, and prompts both an empathic central imagining and a sympathetic acentral imagining.

A third example, one that vividly combines empathic and sympathetic or first-person and third-person perspectives, is from Julian Schnabel's *The Diving Bell and the Butterfly* (2007).[23] The film depicts the tragic and inspiring story of Jean-Dominique Bauby (Mathieu Amalric) (known as Jean-Do), who suffered a stroke in the prime of his life, while driving his son in a sports car in the south of France. He is left all but paralysed as a consequence, having lost the capacity to move physically or communicate verbally, except for his ability to blink, while nonetheless remaining conscious and lucid concerning the world around him (the rare condition of 'locked-in syndrome'). Using a remarkably effective means of conveying bodily POV shots (including a visual framing of these shots with blinking movements and ocular boundaries of Jean-Do's visual field), the film conveys Jean-Do's experience of locked-in syndrome with extraordinary vivacity and realism, contrasting the bodily experience of immobility and inexpressivity (the 'diving bell' sequences, including bodily POV shots) with his mental or conscious freedom, memory and imagination (the 'butterfly' sequences combining imagined or fantasy reveries and images with found footage expressing Jean-Do's state of mind).

During the sequences following his stroke, we empathically 'inhabit' Jean-Do's bodily experiential perspective as he comes to consciousness, discovers the nature of his condition, and attempts to communicate with his ex-lover and mother of his children Céline (Emmanuelle Seigner), therapists Henriette (Marie-Josée Croze) and Marie (Olatz López Garmendia), mistress Inès (Agathe de la Fontaine) and publishing assistant Claude (Anne Consigny), each of whom is seen at different times responding to Jean-Do in direct POV close-up shots emphasizing their expressive faces. Here again (bodily) POV shot sequences double as expressive reaction shots showing the subtle emotional responses to Jean-Do's situation, the three women's powerful attempts to communicate with him despite his all but unimaginable experience of locked-in syndrome. As he embarks on the extraordinary project of dictating his memoirs, his amanuensis painstakingly reciting the alphabet until she reaches the letter Jean-Do wishes to spell out (signalled by the blinking of his 'good' eye), the viewer is given extraordinary access to both Jean-Do's bodily-perceptual and his emotional-reflective experiences (using music, imagined imagery and first-person voiceover in conjunction with the bodily POV shots). Here the striking convergence of POV and reaction shots serves to both convey his bodily perceptual perspective and his emotional, subjective inner state; these sequences foreground the fitful communication of meaning that transpires between Jean-Do and his female interlocutors, which eventually results in his completion of a book manuscript. The latter is finally published just before Jean-Do's death, an event itself depicted from a first-person bodily perspective, Jean-Do receiving a copy of his memoir, *The Diving Bell and the Butterfly*, just before his consciousness fades into light.

Contra Jinhee's Choi's criticism of what Smith takes to be central imagining, which she claims is more typically a perceptual response, involving involuntary perceptual or affective processes (startle reflexes, kinetic and affective mirroring),[24] the cinempathic sequences that I have discussed rely on the interaction between both perceptual-affective and emotional-reflective dimensions. They involve both perceptual imagining combined with more cognitive-reflective imagining in order for us to experience and hence understand both Jean-Do's bodily-perceptual and emotional-imaginative experience as well as the deeply moving expressive responses of the female characters. In the same way that empathy is not merely affective mimicry or emotional contagion (although it also encompasses these phenomena), so too perceptual imagining combines with cognitive or reflective imagining in order to constitute the complex bodily and emotional 'mindreading' necessary to engage with cinematic narrative. *The Diving Bell and the Butterfly* shows how a more embodied conception of cinematic imagination — a cinempathy combining empathic and sympathetic responses and diverse patterns of perspective-taking — allows us to better understand these kind of POV/reaction shot sequences, as well as more conventional forms of character interaction familiar from narrative film.

Cinempathic Imagining

Indeed, such cases suggest that it is not always clear whether central and acentral imagining can be so readily distinguished, although they can nonetheless work with each other in a dynamic, temporally unfolding manner. This is what I have elsewhere called 'cinempathy' as a way of capturing the kinetic, perspective-shifting quality of cinematic imagining.[25] Both empathic first-person imagining and sympathetic third-person imagining come together — or involve sequential forms of perspective-taking — in such cinempathic sequences. Indeed, cinema excels in presenting temporal as well as affective-emotional shifts in perspective combining empathetic and sympathetic, personal/central and impersonal/acentral forms of imagining. In narrative film, moreover, it is not only a matter of expressing the subjective (perceptual as well as emotional) experiences of a character but also of eliciting moral-ethical evaluation of their experience in a given dramatic situation. It is this elicitation of both empathic and sympathetic engagement, solicited via central (empathic) imagining and acentral (sympathetic) imagining unfolding dynamically over time that makes cinematic emotional engagement so experientially rich and ethically complex.

Here I would suggest that such film sequences combine imaginative perspectives in order to enhance sympathetic spectator allegiance via perceptual as well as cognitive alignment, which heightens and intensifies the aesthetic and moral effects of theses sequences. From this point of view, *cinempathic imagining* (dynamically combining both empathic and sympathetic perspectives) can play a decisive role in realizing the ethical potential of film as a medium of ethical experience. Cinempathic imagining complements the 'structure of sympathy', that is the elicitation of moral allegiance for characters, in order to provide experientially 'thick' depictions of ethical responsiveness and social-political complexity. This requires being able to imagine, not just as an abstract thought but as a rich perceptual, emotional and reflective experience, what certain experiences would be like. This in turn enables one to better imagine and thus appreciate their moral salience or ethical import, which means exercising our capacity to perceive and emotionally respond to the moral-ethical experiences of characters with life experiences or perspectives other than one's own — to exercise our moral imaginations. We are able, in short, to better 'cinempathize' with the other.

Smith quotes Kendall Walton who puts the point well: '"In order to understand how minorities feel about being discriminated against, one should imagine not just instances of discrimination but instances of discrimination against *oneself*; one should imagine *experiencing* discrimination."'[26] We need to be able to imagine, in other words, the life experiences of others, especially when those experiences might otherwise remain marginal, ignored or 'invisible' in terms of their experiential recognizability and social visibility. This is one way in which cinematic narrative can contribute to ethical understanding: by providing experientially rich forms of imaginative involvement in the perspectives of others, especially those whose experiences are not part of the ideological status quo. Cinematic narratives can also enable marginalized or minority perspectives to be recognized, not only offering recognition of a minority's experiences of discrimination but exposing those belonging to dominant or majority perspectives to ways of experiencing the world that they may not have been able or willing to acknowledge, whether socially, ethically or politically.

In short, cinempathic imagining, which combines experiential perspective-taking involving both empathic and sympathetic imagining, is a powerful way of depicting and exploring narrative situations involving conflicting or varying experiential perspectives, complex identities and conflicting value perspectives (e.g. in films dealing with racial/ethnic discrimination and the failure or denial of intersubjective recognition). Emphasizing the moral-ethical significance of cinempathic imagining is thus another way of showing how cinema can serve as a medium of ethical experience.

Two Phenomenological Criticisms

Both cognitivist and phenomenological accounts emphasize the role of imagining. This can be understood as empathic central imagining from the viewpoint of a character, or sympathetic acentral imagining from within the diegetic world but not necessarily sharing the viewpoint of the character. We can exercise empathic imagination in ways that both sensitize us to the moral-ethical dimension of (perceptual and emotional) 'mindreading' required in order to understand others, which thereby enables us to expand our horizons of meaning via unfamiliar experiential perspectives. Ethical experience involving emotional simulation, perspective-taking, empathic imagination and affective attunement coupled with cognitive reflection: all of these elements, working together, contribute to the power of cinema as a medium of ethical experience.

Both cognitivist and phenomenological accounts, however, tend to focus on individuated characters, hence they emphasize the 'higher-order' cognitive functions of 'make-believe' or mental simulation elicited by perceptual imaginings or imaginative perceptual props. What this neglects is that individuated characters are not encountered in a neutral context or blank background; rather, they are revealed perceptually *and* cognitively as meaningful or intelligible within an already articulated *cinematic world*. 'Top-down' processes of cognitive imagining or mental simulation presuppose a range of affective, perceptual, embodied 'bottom-up' processes that contribute to the constitution of a plausible and meaningful cinematic world within which such characters can show up as intelligible in the first place. Cinematic imagination is not just mental simulation regarding isolated acts, states or characters; it involves, rather, a suite of affective, perceptual and embodied responses that augment and interact with 'higher-order' processes in order to enrich our apprehension of complex cinematic worlds. Remove the elements or conditions constituting that world — think of the scene in *The Matrix* (1999) where Neo is shown the 'reality' of the computer simulation that he and others take for reality — and we no longer have a meaningful cinematic context in which both central and acentral imagining can function. It is only within a meaningfully articulated fictional world, one structured via the selective composition of audiovisual elements, and that attunes us affectively such that we are primed to respond to that world in appropriate ways, that the game of imaginative simulation or fictional make-believe can get under way.

It is also important to note the role of *perceptual imagining* interacting with *cognitive imagining* in fictional engagement with film. The POV shot sequences that I have discussed all suggest an interplay of personal/central and impersonal/acentral imagining: Smith's examples of the famous dolly-zoom shot of Scottie's experience of vertigo; my examples of Agent Clarice Starling being stalked by serial killer Buffalo Bill in a darkened cellar; the perspective of Manuela's dying son in *All about My Mother*; and Jean-Do's remarkable communicative engagements with his therapist-amanuensis, ex-lover and mistress. All these examples rely on the coalescing or fusion of subjective POV and third-person reaction shots depicting the characters' expressions, responses and actions, and hence are constituted via the superimposition of central/personal and acentral/impersonal imagining. Moreover, each sequence also relies on the interplay of *perceptual* imagining (aligning us with Scottie's visual point of view as he 'sees' or experiences the vertiginous 'collapse' and retreat of the ground below) and *propositional/cognitive* imagining (where we reconstruct and respond to the thought or idea of the situation being depicted, or imagine both the nature of the characters' responses and the meaning or implications of these terrible events).

All four examples are audiovisually arresting, making sound and image work together in intersecting but also dissonant ways (the use of silence, selective aural focus and backgrounded sound in Manuela's stricken cries of grief; the emphasis on Clarice's terrified panting and the ominous click of the gun that Buffalo Bill aims at Clarice; the use of sound and music in conjunction with visual cues in Scottie's experience of vertigo; *The Diving Bell*'s use of bodily cues as well as music and voiceover). All four vignettes showcase the power of cinema to present compelling instances of perceptual imagining, but at the same time show, via the fusion of POV and reaction shot sequences, the ways in which perceptual imagining needs to be contextualized by cognitive or propositional imagining (e.g., the terrible thought of a mother watching her son die before her eyes, or of the son seeing his mother's grief in his last moments before death; the tragic thought of being restricted to communicating one's thoughts and memories via the blinking of one's eye). To separate and isolate perceptual/sensory from cognitive/propositional imagining does not adequately capture the phenomenological experience of overlapping or coalescing of these different dimensions of imagining, so beautifully synthesized in the powerful cinematic sequences that I have analysed.

These examples of cinempathic imagining suggest that we need to articulate a properly *cinematic imagination*: one that captures the dynamic interplay of both these forms of imagining — perceptual and cognitive — which together enable us to perceive, be affectively and emotionally engaged by, and reflect upon cinematic narrative art. The cinematic imagination should be understood as encompassing both perceptual and cognitive aspects or modes of imagining in ways that elicit embodied cognition and moral reflection, perceptual-emotional engagement as well as moral-ethical evaluation. In this respect, the cinematic imagination, understood in both embodied and reflective senses, plays a vital role in our emotional as well as ethical engagement with film.

NOTES

1   Carl Plantinga, *Moving Viewers: American Film and the Spectator's Experience* (Berkeley: University of California Press, 2009); Jane Stadler, *Pulling Focus: Intersubjective Experience, Narrative Film, and Ethics* (New York and London: Continuum, 2008).

2   As I discuss further below, I take empathy and sympathy to be closely related forms of affective and imaginative perspective-taking, the former involving first-person, or personal, imagining, the latter involving third-person, or impersonal, imagining.

3   See Amy Coplan, 'Catching Characters' Emotions: Emotional Contagion Responses to Narrative Fiction Film', *Film Studies: An International Review* 8 (2006), 26–38; Alex Neill, 'Empathy and (Fiction) Film' in *Philosophy of Film and Motion Pictures: An Anthology*, edited by Noël Carroll and Jinhee Choi (Malden, MA: Basil Blackwell, 2006).

4   Jinhee Choi, 'Leaving It Up to the Imagination: POV and Imagining from the Inside', *Journal of Aesthetics and Art Criticism* 63:1 (Winter 2005), 17–25; Sarah Cooper, *Film and the Imagined Image* (Edinburgh: Edinburgh University Press, 2019); Eva M. Dadlez, 'Seeing and Imagination: Emotional Response to Fictional Film', *Midwest Studies in Philosophy* XXXIV (2016), 120–35; Julian Hanich, 'Omission, Suggestion, Completion: Film and the Imagination of the Spectator', *Screening the Past* 43 (2018), http://www.screeningthepast.com/2018/02/omission-suggestion-completion-film-and-the-imagination-of-the-spectator/, consulted 15 July 2019; Rafe McGregor, 'The Problem of Cinematic Imagination', *Contemporary Aesthetics* 10 (2012), https://quod.lib.umich.edu/c/ca/7523862.0010.013?view=text;rgn=main, consulted 6 January 2018; Jane Stadler, 'The Empath and the Psychopath: Ethics, Image, and Intercorporeality in Bryan Fuller's *Hannibal*', *Film-Philosophy* 21:3 (2017), 410–27.

5   See Shen-yi Liao and Tamar Gendler's entry on 'Imagination', *Stanford Encyclopaedia of Philosophy* (2019), https://plato.stanford.edu/entries/imagination/, consulted 15 July 2018.

6   Leslie Stevenson, 'Twelve Conceptions of Imagination', *British Journal of Aesthetics* 43:3 (2003), 238–59.

7   See Jean-Paul Sartre, *The Imaginary: A Phenomenological Psychology of the Imagination*, translated by Jonathan Webber (London and New York: Routledge, 2004).

8   Rafe McGregor, 'The Problem of Cinematic Imagination'. See Choi, 'Leaving It Up to the Imagination', for a good critical discussion of Currie and Smith on POV shots and central imagining.

9   See, for example, Daniel Frampton, *Filmosophy* (London Wallflower Books, 2006), 46–8.

10 Murray Smith, 'Imagining from the Inside' in *Film Theory and Philosophy*, edited by Richard Allen and Murray Smith (Oxford: Oxford University Press, 1997), 412–30. See Choi, 'Leaving It Up to the Imagination', 18–20.

11 Gregory Currie, *Image and Mind* (Cambridge: Cambridge University Press, 1995), 152–5.

12 Smith, 'Imagining from the Inside', 413; Currie, *Image and Mind*, 144.

13 Coplan, 'Catching Characters' Emotions'.

14 Amy Coplan, 'Understanding Empathy: Its Features and Effects' in *Empathy: Philosophical and Psychological Perspectives*, edited by Amy Coplan and Peter Goldie (Oxford: Oxford University Press, 2011), 3–18.

15 Karsten Steuber, 'Empathy', *Stanford Encyclopaedia of Philosophy* (2008/2019) https://plato.stanford.edu/entries/empathy/, 1 November 2019.

16 Shaun Gallagher, *How the Body Shapes the Mind* (Oxford: Oxford University Press, 2005).

17 Dan Zahavi, 'Beyond Empathy: Phenomenological Approaches to Intersubjectivity' in *Phenomenology. Critical Concepts in Philosophy, Vol. II*, edited by M. Dermot and L. Embree (London and New York: Routledge, 2004), 179–200.

18 Smith, 'Imagining from the Inside', 414.

19 Smith, *Engaging Characters*, 81–4.

20 Smith, 'Imagining from the Inside', 416.

21 Currie, *Image and World*, 179–80.

22 Smith, 'Imagining from the Inside', 417.

23 See Jane Stadler, 'Cinema's Compassionate Gaze: Empathy, Affect, and Aesthetics in *The Diving Bell and the Butterfly*' in *Cine-Ethics: Ethical Dimensions of Film Theory, Practice, and Spectatorship*, edited by Jinhee Choi and Mattias Frey, 27–42.

24 Choi, 'Leaving It Up to the Imagination', 19–22.

25 Robert Sinnerbrink, 'Cinempathy: Phenomenology, Cognitivism, and Moving Images', *Contemporary Aesthetics* (16 June 2016), https://www.contempaesthetics.org/newvolume/pages/article.php?articleID=747, consulted 9 December 2018.

26 Smith, 'Imagining from the Inside', 426.

Imitation of Life: Cinema and the Moral Imagination

Jane Stadler

> 'The great instrument of moral good is the imagination.'
> Percy Bysshe Shelley, *A Defence of Poetry* (1821)

There is a peculiar paradox at the crux of debates about imagination and cinema, given that both imagination and fiction film can involve image formation, fantasy or falsification, and the creative projection of possibilities. On the one hand, critics have held that cinema precludes imaginative activity on the part of the audience because the work of the imagination is done for us in the production of images and fantasies on screen.[1] On the other hand, cinema has fuelled fears that imaginative stimulation will lead audiences to sympathize with characters who contravene moral, legal and social values, and to imitate what they see on screen. Indeed, the concern that films can be morally dangerous has served as justification for censorship in the two largest film industries in the world via the American Motion Picture Production Code (1930–67) and India's Central Board of Film Certification (1952–).[2] In response to overarching questions about how imagination is involved in making sense of ethical experience in and through narrative film, this article develops an account of imaginative engagement with cinema, concentrating on the moral imagination as it relates to empathy, ethical perception and imagining others' inner lives. Of particular interest are the deliberative, sensory and emotional aspects of spectators' engagement with characters, and my aim is to develop a more expansive account of the moral imagination that rejects traditional oppositions to reason and embodied understanding in favour of acknowledging imagination's narrative

Paragraph 43.3 (2020): 298–313
DOI: 10.3366/para.2020.0342
© Edinburgh University Press
www.euppublishing.com/para

characteristics and its centrality to thinking and feeling. Following philosopher John Dewey, 'all conscious experience', and aesthetic experience in particular, 'has of necessity some degree of imaginative quality';[3] accordingly, the present study examines how cinematic artworks can illuminate the role of imagination in aesthetic experience and ethical life.

A key principle underpinning the Motion Picture Production Code was that 'No picture will be produced which will lower the moral standards of those who see it'; similarly, the Central Board of Film Certification took up the mission to ensure that 'film does not deprave the morality of the audience'.[4] This demonstrates the extent to which industrial and regulatory frameworks can be anchored to moral strictures that may constrain the creative imagination. The Code was driven by fears about the power of art and imagination, stating: 'Art enters intimately into the lives of human beings. The art of motion pictures has the same object as the other arts — the presentation of human thought, emotion, and experience, in terms of an appeal to the soul through the senses.'[5] This not only highlights what were deemed to be contentious elements of the imagination in relation to film — the appeal to emotions and sensations — it also suggests the centrality of emotion to the moral imagination.

Whether traversing the affective terrain of everyday life or entering the story world of a film, emotions are 'feelings through which we apprehend what matters to us. The embodied phenomenology of emotions is linked with the revelation of value or significance.'[6] Philosopher Mark Johnson contends that ethical values arise from social and cultural experiences, including experiences of film and art, and ethical thinking and understanding involve an embodied, emotional component as well as 'a capacity to explore imaginatively how possible courses of action might enrich meanings, resolve tensions, and expand the scope of our understanding'.[7] Extending Johnson's argument that metaphor is 'the locus of our imaginative exploration of possibilities for action'[8] and that art and literature can cultivate the moral imagination, I examine how cinema elicits what Dewey has termed 'dramatic rehearsal', in which ethical agents use their imaginations to figure out which course of action leads to the best outcome in a particular scenario.[9]

I propose to think through these issues using as a case study Fannie Hurst's popular 1933 novel *Imitation of Life* and its screen adaptations by directors John Stahl (1934) and Douglas Sirk (1959). Unlike the novel or Stahl's film, Sirk's finely wrought melodrama explores concepts of imitation and fantasy via protagonists who are stage performers and whose identities are masked by the roles they play, with self-centred dreams and aspirations leading to a failure of other-oriented empathic imagination. At the same time, through character engagement, the film asks the audience to invest emotionally and imaginatively in moral issues related to race, gender and class that were prominent in the civil rights era and remain significant today.

Out of consideration for growing moral awareness of the rights of African Americans and women, Sirk made several changes to the storyline of the novel and the earlier film, which took place in New Jersey in the 1910s. The original story of *Imitation of Life* follows a white widow, Bea, and her African American nanny and friend, Delilah, as they raise their daughters and develop a restaurant business together, combining Bea's maple syrup with Delilah's waffles.[10] Delilah's daughter, Peola, has inherited such a pale complexion from her fair-skinned Negro father that she is able to pass as white, which brings racial tensions to the surface and leads her to tragically reject Delilah and her own heritage.

The 1934 film was initially prohibited by Production Code enforcers Will Hays and Joseph Breen due to the intimation of miscegenation, the depiction of which was then forbidden.[11] In this era, 'conformity to a white, middle-class, heterosexual American norm became a national obsession, as well as a survival mechanism, especially for those deemed different'.[12] No miscegenation takes place in the plot, but the storyline invites the audience to *imagine* miscegenation in Peola's ancestry and in her future as she attempts to pass as white and assimilate into white society. Infecting the audience's imagination with the suggestion of interracial sex was considered a moral perversion that the Code was meant to censor. Sirk updated the narrative to reflect the social context of New York between 1947 and 1958, casting Lana Turner as Lora, an ambitious actress and mother of Susie (Sandra Dee), and Juanita Moore as Annie, Lora's domestic worker and mother of the fair-skinned Sarah Jane (Susan Kohner).[13] The power of the Code and the aversion to interracial relationships had dissipated somewhat by the time of the film's release in 1959 due to Breen's retirement and landmark court cases that overturned racial segregation.[14] However, studio executives still harboured concerns about white audiences in the Southern states avoiding films about race relations.[15] In the USA in 1959 it was generally unacceptable to depict interracial romance on screen because it was deemed to be immoral and in some states it was still illegal. Sarah Jane's light-skinned Negro father is only mentioned fleetingly and her Caucasian boyfriend, Frankie (played by Troy Donahue), furiously rejects her when he discovers she is African American.

The themes of imitation, images and reflections that imperfectly mirror reality are given form in Sirk's signature use of metaphoric *mise en scène*. For instance, in a scene that could not have been included in the 1934 film due to fears about miscegenation, Sarah Jane surreptitiously meets Frankie late one night and beseeches him, 'Couldn't we run away? I'd do anything to be with you.' The scene takes place in a seedy part of town with piano music from a saloon barely audible in the distance as the couple pause in front of the window of an empty bar for rent, suggestive of vice and a hint of transactional sexuality. The camera pans left, following Frankie's movement away from Sarah Jane as he considers her plan to elope and leans back against the glass window, looking off-screen at her. Although Sarah Jane is now out of shot, the audience can see her reflection beside Frankie in the window as he says, 'Just tell me one thing, is it true?' Sarah Jane's image smiles as she asks naively, 'Is what true?' Frankie leans in menacingly to confront her, and the camera pans right from the reflection to a medium close-up of Sarah Jane's vulnerable face as he raises his voice, looks down on her and aggressively snarls, 'Is your mother a nigger?' At this moment, a percussive tune blares and jarring non-diegetic jazz music conveys tumultuous emotions. Affronted, she replies, 'No, I'm as white as you are!' 'You're lying,' Frankie challenges; 'I'm not,' she shrieks, as we cut to see her reflection in the window backing fearfully away from her vicious beau. Frankie pursues her and beats her brutally, leaving her bleeding and sobbing, collapsed among the trash cans in the alley as tempestuous music underscores his frenzied assault.

Sirk pointedly uses music to communicate the emotionally cacophonous mixture of passion, prejudice and betrayal as he draws attention to Sarah Jane's image, her reflection, to make a distinction between her embodied identity as an African American vulnerable to racism and the deceptive social performance required to pass as white. Sarah Jane's image is her lie, yet it is also her self. In the space that opens up between these two aspects of Sarah Jane's identity, her performance of whiteness is revealed to be a protective mantle — a survival mechanism — the attempt to pass as white is a shield against racial violence and hate speech as well as a misguided means to improve her social standing. The moral lesson is clear: the performance and its unmasking both come at great personal cost and both arise from an unjust social order.[16]

In scenes dramatizing ethical evaluations of characters in this manner, we might ask what role imagination plays, if any, and how film engages the audience's moral imagination. In *Filmosophy*, Daniel Frampton distinguishes between perception and imagination to argue for the widely held view that film audiences do 'not necessarily need their conscious active imagination, only their audio-visual perceptual capacities. The filmgoer's experience seems primarily perceptual rather than imaginative. A film such as *Moulin Rouge* almost completely overwhelms the audience, leaving almost no time or space to imagine.'[17] It is easy to see how Frampton's argument could apply to sensory immersion in Sirk's histrionic music and *mise en scène*, but this would be a fundamental misunderstanding of the evocative qualities of cinema and the imaginative complexity of character engagement that requires us to look beyond the surface of things to discern characters' inner motives and emotions. This, I will argue, is an exercise of the moral imagination as we form internal representations of things that are not immediately present to the senses and harness the imagination in service of deliberation, insight, synthesis, understanding and judgement.

Unpacking the relationship between perception and imagination in *Film and the Imagined Image*, Sarah Cooper articulates connections between images that are perceived on screen and images that are formed or imaginatively transformed in the mind's eye, arguing that film guides and prompts imagination when we are not overwhelmed by audiovisual stimuli.[18] As she focuses on the role of imagination in evoking what is latent or concealed beneath imagery perceived by the eye, Cooper suggests that perception and imagination are 'like the outer material of a garment in relation to its lining'.[19] Although Cooper is not theorizing the moral imagination, her evocative phrase alludes to how audiences glean aesthetic clues when perceiving screen performances that reveal deeper layers of intersubjective insight to the imagination. Similarly, in everyday life, imagination augments attentive perception and explores what lies beneath the body's expressive surface when we interpret voices, emotional cues and behaviour. Whereas Cooper's focus is on imaginative image formation and perception with the inner eye, 'imaging' itself is less central to the moral imagination than discerning the affective and cognitive contours of others' subjectivity. In this sense, the moral imagination is best understood as an act of ethical perception related to empathy and mind reading.

Ethicist John Kekes contends that the moral imagination is important for problem solving and must involve an emotional element,[20] but his conception of the imagination is otherwise somewhat restrictive in its focus on image formation, fantasy and falsification. Kekes concentrates on four functions of imagination:

1. formation of images
2. resourceful problem-solving
3. falsification of some aspect of reality
4. mental exploration of what it would be like to realize particular possibilities.

Moral imagination, Kekes claims, 'belongs to the fourth kind of imaginative activity. It is moral, because one central concern of the agents engaged in it is with evaluating the possibilities they envisage as good or evil.'[21]

As Kekes's list reveals, imagination is often conflated with the production of imagery[22] (function one) or *phantasia*, the realm of fantasy and appearances, which is linked to imitation and illusion (function three). For this reason, imagination has been seen as opposed to reason and has acquired negative associations with mistaken belief, mimesis, and the arts of cinema and theatre — all of which feature prominently in *Imitation of Life*. As Ryan puts it, by changing the characterization and the storyline so that it revolves around Lora and Sarah Jane's appearances and performances in theatre and film, Sirk foregrounds staging and performance throughout *Imitation of Life*.[23] At the same time, the film actively invites and involves the fourth kind of imaginative activity: construing potential actions and evaluating possible outcomes as morally good or bad.

Given the centrality of drama and staged performance, Dewey's thoughts about art, ethics and imagination are pertinent. When considering the nature of ethical deliberation in *Human Nature and Conduct*, Dewey objects to utilitarian moralists who believe that 'judgment about good and evil in action consists in calculation of agreeable and disagreeable consequences, of profit and loss'; instead, he uses the metaphor of theatre to argue that ethical deliberation 'is a dramatic rehearsal (in imagination) of various competing possible lines of action'.[24] I consider that Dewey's work on dramatic rehearsal encompasses resourceful problem solving and the projection of possibilities. Specifically, moral imagination (the fourth function of imagination listed by Kekes) leads to deciding upon the best line of action and the creative resolution of a problem (function two). Furthermore, Kekes unnecessarily restricts the moral imagination to *mental* exploration in a way that sits in tension with his own appreciation of the salience of emotion in ethical understanding. Not only does ethical value and significance have an affective, emotive component that is not purely mental, but dramatic rehearsal implies a form of embodied enactment. Even if enactment takes place in the imagination, it involves the body.

As neuroscientist Vittorio Gallese explains, human cognition is sensory and embodied in nature and recent discoveries identify close connections between cognition, perception and action in ways that have transformed understandings of perception and imagination.[25] Gallese's embodied simulation theory is based on the function of mirror neurons: a neural mirroring mechanism is activated when we perform a gesture or facial expression or feel an emotion or sensation and also when we witness the same action, expression or feeling being performed or experienced by someone else. Importantly, embodied simulation also takes place when we watch films, read novels, listen to stories or 'when we imagine perceiving something or imagine doing something'.[26] Each of these forms of embodied simulation activates mirror neurons and sensory-motor centres of the brain and each aspect has imaginative components. This process of mimicking expressions and mirroring feelings is central to empathizing with others, adopting their position and understanding them from within.[27] The moral imagination involves this 'bottom-up' or involuntary empathy that is catalysed by perceiving expressions, forming emotional sense impressions, or mentally representing images, behaviours and gestures, but empathy also requires 'top-down' processes of position-taking driven by cognition and the ability to 'emotionally represent an experience that is not immediately present to oneself as if it were'.[28] In this sense Dewey's concept of dramatic rehearsal is not just an instructive metaphor for the theatre of life; it aligns with the process of embodied simulation, which is integral to how the imagination functions when perceiving and envisioning human behaviour on or off screen.

In Sirk's cinematic exploration of the moral imagination and its failure in *Imitation of Life*, acting is a part of Lora's and Sarah Jane's professional identities as stage performers, but it is also central to their personal identities and interpersonal interactions as they engage in pretence and deception, whether that means passing as white or wealthy, misleading others, lying outright or evading the truth. Sirk described his film as 'a piece of social criticism — of both black and white'.[29] In this context the theme of performance is directly relevant to identity politics in that Sarah Jane is striving to 'escape her condition' by pretending to be white and 'trying to vanish into the imitation world of vaudeville'; similarly, Lora's own life as a single mother and an actress disconnected from those she loves 'is a very cheap imitation'.[30] Lora's unscrupulous manager offers a sharp character assessment the first time he encounters her during her struggle to find work: 'You lied,' he states. 'All actresses lie. It was a good acting job.'

Imitation of Life has been criticized for featuring demeaning stereotypes and assimilation, yet it does so in ethically multifaceted ways that promote social consciousness. For instance, whereas African American cultural theorist bell hooks critiques the mammy figure, she also reflects on being drawn to the struggle of Peola in the 1934 film as a young woman 'who did not want to be confined by blackness, that "tragic mulatto" who did not want to be negated'.[31] This theme is developed in Sirk's 1959 remake when Sarah Jane attempts to pass as white at school and Lora tells Annie, 'Don't be upset. Children are always pretending. You know that.' Annie responds with moral conviction, 'No, it's a sin to be ashamed of what you are. And it's even worse to pretend and to lie. Sarah Jane has to learn the Lord must have had his reasons for making some of us black and some white. How do you explain to your child she was born to be hurt?'

Sirk's creative use of characterization and dialogue to voice a social criticism is in itself the aesthetic expression of a moral judgement and a call for a more just society. Susan Babbitt's work on the role of fiction and the moral imagination in imagining a better world suggests that, in systematically unjust systems, 'social structures and practices make certain possibilities unimaginable'.[32] By this she means that for people like Sarah Jane and Annie living in a racist culture, the capacity for moral agency is curtailed and we need to look beyond judgements of their actions and choices to the need for social reform and ethical transformation: 'the moral component in questions about individual reasonableness is often a judgment about the moral nature of the society as a whole and hence moral vision of what would constitute a more adequate society.'[33] Sarah Jane's desire to pursue self worth and status in the same ways that a white person could is, in Babbitt's terms, an impossible dream. It is a desire that her mother judges to be morally wrong — sinful — yet it is still an act of moral imagination based on deliberations about justice and reasonable judgements about the socio-moral code. Because Annie's ethic of care situates her at the moral heart of the film and Sarah Jane's actions wound her deeply, the audience would be inclined to judge Sarah Jane harshly if Sirk's own moral vision of society's flaws were not so artfully expressed, revealing how an unjust society can deform character and restrict possibilities for right action.

Sirk's film focuses attention on ethical concerns related to identity politics and encourages reflection on competing moral standpoints, but in order to conceptualize how the moral imagination is activated by cinema, it is necessary to detail how imaginative engagement with films extends beyond narrative comprehension in different media or fables that inform moral understanding.[34] In an insightful article about the film audience's imaginative activity, Julian Hanich demonstrates that cinematic imagination is sensual and that it involves acts of visual and aural completion in response to the filmmaker's artistic elision or evocation of narrative content: 'imagining fills in and enriches what the film's visuals or its soundtrack both conceal and allude to.'[35] Thus, in *Imitation of Life*, the audience is prompted to imagine Sarah Jane's father when his fair-skinned appearance is referred to and perhaps to wonder whether her great-grandfather may have been a white slave owner as we seek to fill in the backstory. Omissions in the narrative provide a portal for the imagination to elaborate on the diegetic world. Likewise, Cooper states that 'the presence of an absence that prompts the creation of a mental image that supplements what is on screen is an integral part of how film stimulates the imagination.'[36] Drawing on the work of phenomenologist Maurice Merleau-Ponty, Cooper makes the important point that the audience's mental activity when watching films cannot be separated from our sensual and embodied engagement with cinema and the intertwined nature of imagination and perception as intentional activities.[37]

The understanding of moral imagination that I advance here couples this phenomenological perspective with neuroscientific research into embodied simulation and cognitive-philosophical approaches to film and art. For instance, cognitivist Murray Smith argues that artistic representations of empathy scenarios, such as those found in narrative films, provide elaborate examples of moral imagining that may enhance the reach, scale and intensity of empathy.[38] Similarly, Johnson's research into cognitive science and moral philosophy shows that art and narrative fiction are important channels for developing the empathic dimensions of the ethical imagination because they require us to imagine other people's lives and take up their perspectives with sensitivity to context, feeling and detail.[39] Johnson argues that ethical thinking and understanding are tied to emotions and that moral deliberation is 'a form of embodied, embedded, enactive problem solving that requires a capacity to explore imaginatively how possible courses of action might enrich meanings, resolve tensions, and expand the scope of our understanding'.[40] In narrative film, each aesthetic and technical choice has consequences for the audience in terms of perceptual alignment and emotional or ethical allegiance with the subjects on screen, as Smith's work demonstrates. This gets to the heart of why emotional and empathic engagement with cinema can be such a rich imaginative experience.

Well-crafted melodramas thematize the characters' emotional predicaments, moral quandaries and psychological dramas in ways that involve the 'sublimation of dramatic conflict into décor, colour, gesture, and composition of frame'.[41] Sirk himself claims that camera angles and lighting choices can represent a film director's thoughts and philosophical perspective,[42] and in *Imitation of Life* the invocation of allusive *mise en scène* and visual metaphors is evident when Annie watches her daughter perform at a nightclub under the assumed name of Linda, dancing on stage between masks that signify theatre and drama. When Annie visits her daughter after the show, Sarah Jane turns her back on her mother and appraises her own pale reflection in a dressing table mirror, stating, 'I'm somebody else. I'm white.' She breaks down sobbing as her mother's careworn reflection looks on silently in the background before Annie embraces her warmly, her own soulful dark eyes welling with tears. This tender moment of reconciliation is interrupted by yet another occasion for imitation when a guest mistakes Annie for a maid; in order to avoid revealing Sarah Jane's identity, Annie pretends to be 'Miss Linda's mammie' instead of Sarah Jane's mother. The desolate grief of a mother and daughter torn apart by prejudice is captured first in shots of Sarah Jane's performance and image; then later with stirring non-diegetic violins and empathic close-ups dramatizing the cruelty of racial discrimination that rends the uniting bonds of emotion and humanity. Unbeknown to her daughter, Annie knows that she is dying and in their final embrace expressive close-ups reveal the characters' inner emotional experience, providing the audience with subjective insight and eliciting affective mirroring.[43] Philosopher and film scholar Robert Sinnerbrink contends that in addition to attending to a film's narrative content or the ethical dilemmas, issues and scenarios it represents, we must also relate them to the socio-cultural and ideological context and consider the way events are presented aesthetically.[44] I agree with Sinnerbrink that 'a response brought about by aesthetic means', such as Sirk's use of reflections and visual metaphors, the emotionally laden score, and attentive focus on performance in close-up, 'can broaden our ethical horizons and complicate our moral understanding by way of the ethical experience afforded through film'.[45]

Metaphors of moral vision connect insight and the formation of mental images to moral agency and offer an expanded account of ethical perception that acknowledges the significance of emotion, as typified by Iris Murdoch's moral philosophy.[46] In *The Sovereignty of the Good*, Murdoch focuses on the particulars of everyday experience and articulates conflicting perspectives on the role of imagination in ethics. When Murdoch writes, 'as moral agents we have to try to see justly, to overcome prejudice, to avoid temptation, to control and curb the imagination, to direct reflection',[47] she is concerned that imaginative activity might distract from attending to salient ethical details in a particular person's situation. However, Murdoch's concept of moral vision does include a positive, illuminating role for the imagination: 'clear vision is a result of moral imagination and moral effort' and imagination can help flesh out a picture of the world formed by 'realistic vision with compassion'.[48] Indeed, as the ethically nuanced vision of the human condition offered in Murdoch's novels and her use of imaginative examples in moral philosophy demonstrates, art and narrative cultivate imaginative capabilities that are vital for understanding others. As she brings Murdoch's philosophical writings into dialogue with a selection of films by 'thinking about film as moral philosophy, and the role of film in our individual moral thinking and training', Lucy Bolton argues that 'paying attention to art is a way of developing our moral visions and becoming better people'.[49] Drawing together Murdoch's moral philosophy, Bolton's insights about film and Sinnerbrink's attunement to social context and screen aesthetics, we may come to see in a more ethical way if we patiently pay attention to troubled characters like Sarah Jane and the social circumstances with which they struggle.[50]

To conclude, the moral imagination involves practical reason and creative problem-solving in response to morally complex scenarios, typically involving a narrative dimension and the practice that Dewey terms dramatic rehearsal. Narration is salient because it captures the temporal quality of the moral imagination — the capacity to reflect on past actions and forecast future outcomes, weighing up causation and consequence. By extension, aesthetic experience and the narrative arts are important means for cultivating the moral imagination. I have argued that cinema has a special role to play in fostering the moral imagination and also in understanding how imagination operates. This is partly due to film's narrative form, which can convey moral lessons; however, film's appeal to the senses is equally significant as this facilitates empathic character engagement akin to the way we respond to people in everyday life, reacting to and mirroring the emotions they express. Recent neuropsychological and philosophical research has debunked the claim that we do not need to exercise the imagination when watching films because we perceive the characters and events on screen. Although the imagination can conjure imagery of that which is not present, imagination is not dependent on the strength or clarity of mental visual images and the imagination finds many lacunae to fill when immersed in a film. By bringing neuroscience into dialogue with the humanities, Gallese's ground-breaking work has revealed that the multisensory aesthetic form of cinematic narratives offers insight into embodied, emotive aspects of imagination that have frequently been overlooked in favour of the conscious, top-down acts of deliberation, position taking and judgement. The phenomenological, felt quality of understanding the other from within is an important aspect of embodied simulation that illuminates the bottom-up processes of the embodied imagination and discloses important links to perception. To imaginatively construct inferences and synthesize associations, and to simulate possible consequences is central to ethical deliberation and to the cultivation of moral insights associated with the intentional top-down cognitive processes of empathy. Both conscious and involuntary processes are involved in the moral imagination as we grapple with the ambiguity of others' motives and struggle to find ethically appropriate responses to overwhelming issues such as structural injustice that cause fissures in human character and interpersonal relationships, as Sirk's melodrama reveals. The moral imagination involves drawing on imaginative and ethical resources to interpret metaphors and discern the moral of a story, deliberate about the right course of action in our own lives and the lives other people and characters lead, seek insight into another's motives and evaluate the outcomes of their choices and actions. The aesthetic richness and narrative complexity of morally engaging films can stimulate the imaginative leap required to envision a more just and compassionate world in which diversity is valued and there is an openness to looking at matters from different perspectives and caring about others' points of view.

NOTES

1 See, for example, Daniel Frampton, *Filmosophy* (London: Wallflower, 2006); Roger Scruton, 'Fantasy, Imagination and the Screen', *Grazer Philosophische Studien* 19:1 (1983), 35–46; Malcolm Turvey, 'Imagination, Simulation, and Fiction', *Film Studies* 8 (2006), 116–25.

2 I am grateful to Carl Plantinga for raising important points about the Production Code and film certification while discussing this article. He develops related points in *Screen Stories: Emotion and the Ethics of Engagement* (Oxford: Oxford University Press, 2018), 15–18 (27).

3 John Dewey, 'The Challenge to Philosophy' in *Art as Experience* (New York: Perigee Books, 2005 [1934]), 283. As Steven Fesmire's illuminating account of Dewey's work indicates, 'moral thinking is embodied, aesthetic, encultured, temporal, historical, and communal' (534). Fesmire, 'Morality as Art: Dewey, Metaphor, and Moral Imagination', *Transactions of the Charles S Peirce Society: A Quarterly Journal in American Philosophy* 35:3 (1999), 527–50.

4 'Motion Picture Production Code' (1930), https://www.asu.edu/courses/fms200s/total-readings/MotionPictureProductionCode.pdf, consulted 31 October 2018, 593–96 (594); Central Board of Film Certification of India (1952–), https://www.cbfcindia.gov.in/main/guidelines.html consulted 31 October 2018.

5 'Production Code', 594.

6 Rick Furtak, *Knowing Emotions: Truthfulness and Recognition in Affective Experience* (Oxford: Oxford University Press, 2018), 48.

7 Mark Johnson, *Embodied Mind, Meaning, and Reason: How Our Bodies Give Rise to Understanding* (Chicago: University of Chicago Press, 2017), 227.

8 Mark Johnson, *Moral Imagination* (Chicago: University of Chicago Press, 1993), 35.

9 John Dewey, 'The Nature of Deliberation' in *Human Nature and Conduct: An Introduction to Social Psychology* (New York: Modern Library, 1922), 189–98.

10 Delilah makes pancakes in the 1934 film.

11 See Susan Courtney, 'Picturizing Race: Hollywood's Censorship of Miscegenation and Production of Racial Visibility Through *Imitation of Life*', *Genders* 27 (1998), https://www.colorado.edu/gendersarchive1998-2013/1998/05/01/picturizing-race-hollywoods-censorship-miscegenation-and-production-racial-visibility, consulted 31 October 2018.

12 Harry Benshoff and Sean Griffin, *Queer Images: A History of Gay and Lesbian Film in America* (Lanham: Rowman & Littlefield, 2006), 86.

13   As children, Susie is played by Terry Burnham and Karin Dicker plays Sarah Jane.

14   In *Brown v. Board of Education of Topeka* (1954), the Supreme Court ruled that the segregation of children was not permitted in public schools. It was not until *Loving v. Virginia* in 1967 that state laws prohibiting miscegenation and interracial marriage were ruled by the Supreme Court to be unconstitutional. A film of the latter court case, *Loving*, was directed by Jeffrey Nichols (2016).

15   Tom Ryan, 'Obsessions, Imitations & Subversions, Part Two — on *Imitation of Life*', *Senses of Cinema* 77 (2015), http://sensesofcinema.com/2015/feature-articles/imitation-of-life-adaptations/, consulted 8 December 2018.

16   Regarding passing, see Monique Rooney, 'What Passes in *Imitation of Life* (1959)?', *Humanities Research* 16:1 (2010), 55–77.

17   Frampton goes on to contrast 'the imaginative leap we take at the beginning of the filmgoing experience, with the then non-imaginative engagement with the film' (*Filmosophy*, 154). Engaging with actors playing fictional characters as though they are real people involves an act of make-believe, and that is the only sense in which Frampton thinks audiences imaginatively engage with film. Other scholars like Turvey also disagree 'that engaging with a fiction involves imagining its content' ('Imagination', 124). According to Turvey, we cannot imagine the content of a film because imagination consists of 'thoughts about the possible rather than the actual'; consequently, we can only imagine elements that do not actually appear such as events that happen between scenes ('Imagination', 124).

18   Sarah Cooper, *Film and the Imagined Image* (Edinburgh: Edinburgh University Press, 2019), 21.

19   Cooper, *Film and the Imagined Image*, 26.

20   John Kekes, 'Moral Imagination, Freedom, and the Humanities', *American Philosophical Quarterly* 28:2 (1991), 101–11. To understand a moral agent's motives and actions, Kekes rightly states that we require insight into the emotional drivers informing their choices: 'understanding significance can not be merely cognitive, it must also have a large affective component capable of conveying the appeal the relevant possibilities had for the agent. Thus, we need cognitively and affectively informed imagination to re-create the richness of the possibilities whose significance we want to understand' (102).

21   Kekes, 'Moral Imagination', 101.

22   Elsewhere, I demonstrate the limitations of accounts of imagination primarily concerned with visual image formation. Internal imagery can be evoked for all the senses to different degrees and, although most people can rehearse complex conversations in the voice of their mind, it is more challenging to visualize with vividness and detail. See Jane Stadler, 'Imagination: Inner Sight and Silent Voices' in *Pulling Focus: Intersubjective Experience, Narrative Film and Ethics* (New York: Continuum, 2008), 168–96. As psychologist Joel Pearson states, 'Typically, in imagery generation, we are combining different content

that our senses have previously been exposed to and is stored in our memory.' Joel Pearson, 'The Human Imagination: The Cognitive Neuroscience of Visual Mental Imagery', *Nature Reviews Neuroscience* 20 (2019), 624–34 (625). It is particularly hard to imagine something you have never seen, heard, felt, tasted, smelled or touched. Rather than forging mental copies of sense impressions like an imitation of life, imagining often entails feeling impressions that vary in strength and precision, ranging from aphantasia, which refers to the inability to form mental images, to hyperphantasia, which is photorealistic or eidetic imagery that few people experience (Pearson, 'Human Imagination', 632).

23 Ryan, 'Obsessions, Imitations', 2015.

24 Dewey, *Human Nature and Conduct*, 190. In *Theory of the Moral Life* (New York: Irvington Publishers, 1960), Dewey elaborates: 'Deliberation is actually an imaginative rehearsal of various courses of conduct', and he goes on to detail how imagination is involved in rehearsing potential actions during ethical deliberation, stating, 'we find ourselves in imagination in the presence of the consequences that would follow' (135).

25 Vittorio Gallese, 'Embodied Simulation: Its Bearing on Aesthetic Experience and the Dialogue between Neuroscience and the Humanities', *Gestalt Theory* 41:2 (2019), 113–28.

26 Gallese, 'Embodied Simulation', 116.

27 Gallese, 'Embodied Simulation', 116.

28 Mavis Biss, 'Moral Imagination, Perception, and Judgment', *Southern Journal of Philosophy* 52:1 (2014), 4.

29 John Halliday, *Sirk on Sirk: Conversations with John Halliday* (London: Faber & Faber, 1971), 150.

30 Halliday, *Sirk on Sirk*, 151.

31 bell hooks, *Reel to Real: Race, Sex and Class at the Movies* (London: Routledge, 1996), 203–4.

32 Susan Babbitt, *Impossible Dreams: Rationality, Integrity and the Moral Imagination* (Colorado: Westview Press: 1996), 3.

33 Babbitt, *Impossible Dreams*, 7.

34 See Plantinga, *Screen Stories*, 85. See also Lucy Bolton, *Contemporary Cinema and the Philosophy of Iris Murdoch* (Edinburgh: Edinburgh University Press, 2019). According to Bolton, 'Film can act as a moral fable, which challenges our tendencies to judge and simplify, as well as to examine our own moral vision' (74).

35 Julian Hanich, 'Omission, Suggestion, Completion: Film and the Imagination of the Spectator', *Screening the Past* 43 (2018), http://www.screeningthepast.com/2018/02/omission-suggestion-completion-film-and-the-imagination-of-the-spectator/, consulted 17 August 2019.

36 Cooper, *Imagined Image*, 112.

37   Sarah Cooper, 'Merleau-Ponty and Film: Documenting the Imagination' in *Understanding Merleau-Ponty, Understanding Modernism*, edited by Ariane Mildenberg (London: Bloomsbury Academic, 2018), 157–69 (167).

38   Murray Smith, *Film, Art, and the Third Culture: A Naturalized Aesthetics of Film* (London: Oxford University Press, 2017), 177–97.

39   Mark Johnson, *The Aesthetics of Meaning and Thought: The Bodily Roots of Philosophy, Science, Morality, and Art* (Chicago: University of Chicago Press, 2018), 166.

40   Johnson, *Embodied Mind*, 227.

41   Thomas Elsaesser, 'Tales of Sound and Fury: Observations on the Family Melodrama' in *Film Genre Reader II*, edited by Barry Keith Grant (Austin: University of Texas Press, 1995), 350–80.

42   Halliday, *Sirk on Sirk*, 40.

43   Plantinga, *Screen Stories*, 27. Like Plantinga's work on facial feedback and emotional contagion, Bolton focuses on film's ability to capture and hold attention on emotional performances revealed in close-ups of the human face (*Contemporary Cinema*, 13–14). For Bolton, 'images, pictures and metaphors are at the heart of our imaginations and our contemplation' (205) and this aesthetic capacity to stimulate and expand the imagination enables film to foster empathic insight and augment moral perception.

44   Robert Sinnerbrink, 'Emotional Engagement and Moral Evaluation: Exploring Cinematic Ethics' in *Social Aesthetics and Moral Judgment: Pleasure, Reflection and Accountability*, edited by Jennifer McMahon (London: Routledge, 2018), 196–212.

45   Sinnerbrink, 'Emotional Engagement', 210.

46   For a lucid overview of approaches to the moral imagination, see Biss, 'Moral Imagination', 3. See also Martha Nussbaum, *Love's Knowledge: Essays on Philosophy and Literature* (New York: Oxford University Press, 1990).

47   Iris Murdoch, *The Sovereignty of the Good* (London: Routledge, 1970), 40.

48   Murdoch, *The Sovereignty of the Good*, 37 and 87.

49   Bolton, *Contemporary Cinema*, 7 and 1.

50   Bolton, *Contemporary Cinema*, 40.

Perceptual-Imaginative Space and the Beautiful Ecologies of Rose Lowder's *Bouquets*

Sarah Cooper

Throughout her *Bouquets* series, which she began in 1994, experimental filmmaker Rose Lowder has turned increasingly to the portrayal of specific subjects in ecological places, with flowers as her central point of focus. She notes that her love of flora has led people to ask her whether there are not more important things to do today than to make films about flowers, reporting that she would answer them with a question: 'are there really more important things?'[1] Emphasizing the dependency of bees on flowers and the essential link in the food chain they provide, she affirms how such a subject is not only relevant for her as a filmmaker but also vital to life. In keeping with this, the production of the *Bouquets* is rooted in a concern for the environment. *Bouquets 1–10* (1994–5) were made from 16mm film stock left over from other projects that Lowder did not want to go to waste — an economy of means key to her ecological principles. She used the stock to film anything that she found interesting in a place that she was just passing through, and predominantly it was the flowers in those places that caught her eye. Lowder added to these initial films with two further series: *Bouquets 21–30* (2001–5) and *Bouquets 11–20* (2005–9).[2] There is a seasonal unity to all three series (they are filmed in spring or summer), and each film is roughly a minute in length (1,440 frames), made in-camera and not edited after it has been shot. In the latter two series the images are from organic farms and ecological gardens, mainly in France but also neighbouring countries of Switzerland and Italy. Made in this way relatively close to home, Lowder's work has a low carbon footprint, and she lives by these standards too, buying and eating local produce, and mindful of sustainability wherever possible.[3]

Paragraph 43.3 (2020): 314–329
DOI: 10.3366/para.2020.0343
© Edinburgh University Press
www.euppublishing.com/para

In spite of their name, then, Lowder's *Bouquets* are not the filmic equivalent of the eponymous floral arrangements that are an everyday part of the global mass-market cut flower industry. Rather, they stand apart from mainstream commercial culture as experimental works on perception that attend to wild or organically grown flowers still in their soil. Yet these flowers filmed in situ reach out from the environments in which they grow into the realm of aesthetics: as such, Lowder's bouquets of images open onto an appreciation of beauty that stretches from nature into art and has a long historical lineage. The *Bouquets* constitute an assortment of images configured in such a way that the spectator's involvement is essential to their making, their beauty a function of perceptual production in conjunction with the film apparatus. Lowder's experiments with perception forge in turn a hitherto unexplored connection to imagination that proves crucial to understanding how beauty entwines with ecological commitment — both her own and that which might be stirred in viewers upon watching her films. In this article, I bring imagination explicitly into discussion of her experiments with visual perception as I trace the creation of a perceptual-imaginative space from her early work onwards, attending to questions of beauty and balance that inform the ecologies of her *Bouquets*.

Forming Perceptual-Imaginative Space

Born in Miraflores, near Lima, with a fine art background acquired through her studies first in Peru and then London from the early 1950s to the mid-1960s, Lowder began her career in the film industry working as an editor in London and Paris from the mid-1960s to the early 1970s, before turning to concentrate on her own experimental practice from her home in Avignon in the south of France.[4] In her doctoral thesis, nominally supervised by Jean Rouch and completed in 1987, Lowder makes the point that it is only by setting aside intentions that are either purely expressive or aesthetic that experimental film can explore the perception of the sensible world.[5] Fittingly, she began her experimental film work on visual perception without a camera, punching holes in pieces of 16mm filmstrip and drawing lines on them directly with a marker pen, captivated by the difference between what could be seen on the strip and what then appeared on screen when the strip was run through a projector. These *Boucles/Loops* (1976–7) served as her starting point for advancing further experiments with perception, now using a camera and filming a range of subjects. Before I address the perceptual explorations of Lowder's *Bouquets*, it is useful first to consider an early work that paved the way towards the series, since it enables us to glimpse the emergence of a relation to imagination that will be important throughout my ensuing discussion.

Rue des Teinturiers (1979) is one of Lowder's earliest films made with a camera and is her first treatment of a vegetal subject. She set up her camera on her small balcony on rue des Teinturiers in Avignon in order to shoot the foliage of a laurel on the balcony and the street behind it over a period of six months, alternating between focusing on plant and street, figure and background.[6] When projected, the film bears some similarity to structural film form as defined by P. Adams Sitney with reference to US films of the 1960s, due to the persistent vibrating or flickering effect generated by filmmaking and projection.[7] The quivering quality was to dominate many of her other films, including the *Bouquets* series, and in Lowder's practice it comes from the fact that she filmed one frame at a time on her 16mm film stock and changed the focus for each frame. The camera is entirely static throughout the filming process, but when the images are projected, the changes of focus seen in swift succession generate the rapid movements that give rise to a composite image of the filmed elements, such that there is no superimposition but rather individual frames mixing instead. When speaking of a later film, *Tournesols/Sunflowers* (1982), Lowder describes how the viewer's perceptual mechanism contributes to this effect: 'Due to the varying time-lengths our perceptual system needs to treat different types of visual stimulus, parts of images situated on separate frames are seen, under certain circumstances, depending on the graphic and plastic features of the successive frames, to appear simultaneously or as overlapping each other on the screen.'[8] For Lowder the smallest unit of film is smaller than the frame. The effects of perception in response to her films lead to the mind creating more than is visible frame by frame in a more complex manner than was discernible in her initial, camera-less *Boucles*. On the strip of *Rue des Teinturiers* there are clearly discernible individual images but when run through the projector, the film stock coupled with the perceptual mechanism of the spectator gives rise to a viewing experience of a visual palimpsest. The effect of filming and projecting the plant and the street in this manner means that shots of the plant give way to shots of the street and, at times, albeit momentarily, viewers see through the plant to its other side whereas in ordinary perception this would, of course, be impossible since what is behind the plant would have to be imagined instead.

As Lowder notes in her doctoral thesis, one of the aims of *Rue des Teinturiers* was to use the filmic apparatus to gain access to elements present in reality that would otherwise have remained imperceptible.[9] Her reference points in her research into perception are many and varied, with visual perception of movement and colour forming a main area of enquiry supported by scholarly research on the topic published in the early 1970s.[10] Her experimentation with perception chimes with the philosophical explorations of early twentieth-century phenomenologists, too. Lowder's filming of the laurel and the street reveals that it is necessary ordinarily to move around three-dimensional objects in space and time in order to perceive them and what lies behind them, as both Jean-Paul Sartre and Maurice Merleau-Ponty would concur in their now-classic work. In the work of Sartre and Merleau-Ponty, differing elaborations of the phenomenology of perception in the visible world broach nonetheless a relation to what cannot be seen, and a cube is one of the emblematic objects for their observations.[11] For Sartre, the perception of a cube, like other objects, signifies '[t]he necessity of *making a tour* of objects, of waiting, as Bergson said, until the "sugar dissolves"'.[12] For Merleau-Ponty, it is by conceiving of his body as a mobile object that he is able to interpret perception and construct the cube whose sides are not visible to him without moving around it.[13] For Lowder, it is the camera that permits access to an eventual vision of what is normally invisible at specific moments in time from fixed vantage points but without moving around what it films. Through the intricate filming of the laurel, followed by the combined effects of projection and spectatorial perception, Lowder enables viewers to see multiple things in the same space and to see through solids — here the laurel — to what lies beyond them. The space mapped from the perceptible to the imperceptible relies on a point of contact established with what can normally only be imagined from a given standpoint. It is not that Lowder activates imagining in the sense that spectators conjure mental images of what is not there.[14] Rather, the spatial structure is that of both perception and imagination, due to the impossible perspectives created on the basis of what is seen.

Lowder's filming of the laurel on her balcony is necessarily more restricted in spatial terms than the filming of her *Bouquets* will be as she roams across many different sites. Moreover, between *Rue des Teinturiers* and the later series, Lowder will also make other films that explore perception and that feature flowers and blossoms in more expansive spaces, from peach blossom in an orchard (*Champ provençal/Provencal Field* (1979)) through to sunflowers in a field (*Les Tournesols/Sunflowers* and *Les Tournesols colorés/Coloured Sunflowers* (1982–3)). The presence of flowers heralds the arrival of beauty in abundance, and the very filmic vision that gave rise to perceiving what could normally only be imagined beyond ordinary sightlines can now invite reflection on its pleasures in the light of an array of colourful, quivering petals. The floral images call for the spatial discussion of perception and imagination to be opened out to broader historical associations formed between imagination, pleasure and beauty — in nature and art — but these will lead back eventually to the connection between the geometrical cuboid shape in the twentieth-century phenomenologists' reflections and Lowder's perceptual-imaginative space.

There may not be much that links the differing reflections of the twentieth-century phenomenologists on perceiving and imagining to the eighteenth-century philosopher Joseph Addison's talk of imagination, but the insistence on a link to vision is something they share, especially in the case of Merleau-Ponty. In his late text 'Eye and Mind', Merleau-Ponty asserts that imagining 'borrows from vision and employs means we owe to it'.[15] Addison focuses more specifically on what he terms the pleasures of the imagination, but insists that they proceed from sight. He positions imagination between sense and understanding, saying that its pleasures derive principally from seeing what is '*great, uncommon, or beautiful*'.[16] These pleasures divide into two categories: primary pleasures that are from objects before the eyes and secondary pleasures from objects that are not actually before the eyes but called up by memories or visions of absent or fictitious things.[17] The play of absence and presence characteristic of much imaginative activity as described through the ages inheres within that play of the invisible and visible also evident in Merleau-Ponty's attention to the cube, in so far as something that is not before the eyes is brought forth in a manner that owes something to vision. The reason why Addison is of particular interest here as I turn to consider Lowder's filmed flowers is not just that he lauded the pleasures of the imagination prompted by beauty, but that he was writing on imagination in relation to beauty at a turning point in the eighteenth century just before other philosophers — most notably Edmund Burke and Immanuel Kant — would introduce a distinction between the beautiful and the sublime. Whereas beauty stimulates the pleasures of the imagination in unalloyed fashion in Addison's work, imagination was to be overwhelmed by the sublime.

When Kant writes in an early series of reflections on the distinction between the feeling of the beautiful and the sublime, a natural scene that may have been spoken about as all of a piece by Addison in terms of the pleasures of the imagination is now divided: 'Lofty oaks and lonely shadows in sacred groves are sublime, flowerbeds, low hedges, and trees trimmed into figures are beautiful.'[18] In the later *Critique of Judgment*, and from the magnitude of the mathematical sublime to the might of the dynamic sublime, Kant affirms a bond that will abide thereafter between the feeling of the sublime and the imagination's inadequacy.[19] The aesthetic power of judging the beautiful refers the imagination in its free play to understanding, whereas in judging a thing sublime it refers the imagination to reason.[20] In the former, imagination and understanding are in accordance; in the latter, imagination and reason are in conflict.[21] There is thus an agitation to the mind in presenting the sublime in nature, but in an aesthetic judgement of the beautiful in nature the mind is in restful contemplation.[22] Although the beautiful was never intentionally downgraded to a secondary position through discussion of the sublime, the influence of the distinction led to a hierarchy in the attention paid to each in years to come such that in the late twentieth century, as cultural scholar Elaine Scarry notes, talk of beauty waned in the Humanities to be replaced by a fascination with the sublime.[23] Alongside beauty, imagination is also displaced when the sublime is privileged. The magnitude and might that the imagination was faced with determined its adequacy.[24] To turn now to Lowder's *Bouquets*, the proportions of her flowers will loom as large on screen as mountains at times, and the quivering dissonance of the images will seem to agitate rather than encourage contemplation; as Guinevere Narraway notes, Lowder's films do not appear to generate the harmony of Kant's conception of the beautiful in nature, *Naturschöne*.[25] But they still maintain a link to the beautiful in which Addison, Burke, and Kant found pleasure in their earlier historical context, in nature and in art, albeit in defamiliarized form. Contemplative harmony may be challenged in the form of her films but a different kind of balance is achieved in the process, which is crucial to her ecological vision. Furthermore, the distinctive perceptual-imaginative space already formed in *Rue des Teinturiers* expands in the *Bouquets* to suggest that there is more to this filmic encounter with floral beauty than meets the eye.

Just Beautiful Bouquets?

Whenever I have presented conference papers on Lowder's *Bouquets*
or had conversations about her films, people have commented most
frequently on how beautiful her work is, even as they note the
challenge of viewing its vibration and flicker. Were appreciation of her
filmed flowers to stop at an aesthetic judgement, the environmental
import of the work would risk getting lost. Some might say that this
does not matter, but thinking back to the ecological principles that
inform their production as well as her lifestyle beyond her filmmaking,
a response to these films that cuts off responsibility to the environments
in which they were made seems a distortion of her practice. An
appreciation of the beauty of her filmed flowers can, however, lead
viewers towards rather than away from ecological commitment. This
move is founded in the specificity of Lowder's treatment of perceptual-
imaginative space, and Scarry clears the path for us to understand and
make such a journey.

Following her observation that the Humanities shifted their interest
to the sublime in the late 1990s, Scarry notes that the Sciences, in
contrast, still featured discussion of 'beautiful' solutions to problems
and 'pretty' theories.[26] Scarry's overriding interest in this work that
originally took the form of her 1997–98 Tanner Lectures on Human
Values is in how beauty might lead to justice. She cites two friends
who respond to her research question, summarizing their observations
with the assumption that they both share: 'beautiful things give rise
to the notion of distribution, to a lifesaving reciprocity, to fairness
not just in the sense of loveliness of aspect but in the sense of "a
symmetry of everyone's relation to one another".'[27] The beauty of
the scientific subjects that seek truth is connected to a sense of fairness
that spans definitions of the beautiful and the just. For Scarry, equality
and symmetry of measure — what for classical philosophers was
epitomized in the shape of the sphere but that I suggest could also
encompass the cube — lead from geometrical shapes into the realm
of justice. Even though we seem to have travelled some distance from
the cube of the phenomenologists, it is by re-establishing a connection
to matters of geometry and equal measure that it is possible to move
from the beautiful to the just in ecological terms, indebted to that
perceptual-imaginative spatial bond that Lowder first lays bare in *Rue
des Teinturiers*. By expanding the human–centred relationship of 'a
symmetry of everyone's relation to one another' so that it becomes
one in which the human and other forms of life entwine, Lowder's

Bouquets create symmetries that lead from beauty to a just relationship with the environment.

Beauty, for Scarry, invites and even requires acts of replication — it inspires a desire to bring copies of itself into being, inciting a gamut of activities from human reproduction to artistic creation.[28] While Lowder's *Bouquets* are non-mimetic versions of the reality of the flowers that she perceives with the naked eye prior to filming, they still bear the trace of their inspiration. These are painstakingly crafted works, and experimental film scholar Enrico Camporesi notes indeed how Lowder's exploration of botanical imagery is also a means of producing ornamental motifs.[29] Indebted to the *plein air* tradition of leaving the studio and going out into nature, and possessing a colour palette sensibility that she attributes to her childhood in Peru, Lowder's is a painterly inheritance and she speaks of an effect akin to pointillism in relation to her *Bouquets*.[30] The beauty of her *Bouquets* pertains, however, to both the floral source and the experimentation that results from the camera and spectator's perceptual systems working with one another to process the films. For Scarry, 'Beauty seems to place requirements on us for attending to the aliveness or (in the case of objects) quasi-aliveness of our world, and for entering into its protection.'[31] As Lowder places her filmed flowers in the field of human regard, she engages in the activity that beauty assists us with, according to Scarry — addressing injustice by requiring of us 'constant perceptual acuity'.[32] Scholarship on Lowder's work has noted the importance of her perceptual explorations with regard to her botanical subject matter. Both Scott MacDonald and Guinevere Narraway have connected Lowder's ecological ethic to what MacDonald terms elsewhere in relation to ecocinema 'a retraining of perception' that engages the viewer in seeing the world differently.[33] The need to alter perception is recognized more widely within contemporary ecophilosophy. In her work with philosopher Michael Marder on the vegetal world, feminist philosopher Luce Irigaray argues that a change in perception is necessary in order to be able to approach coexistence with plants in a meaningful way.[34] It is through further exploration of perceptual–imaginative space that Lowder broaches this question of coexistence in her *Bouquets*.

As with the filming of *Rue des Teinturiers*, the *Bouquets* reveal perceptual-imaginative spatial palimpsests, which allow viewers to see through solid entities to their other side, but they also grant access to something filmed in another place at a different time. In the intervening period between *Rue des Teinturiers* and the making of the first *Bouquets*, Lowder had attempted to reduce the degree of vibration apparent in the earlier work and also to combine this with other techniques. Her way of working was similar to the approach she used in a couple of prior films, *Impromptu* (1989) and *Quiproquo* (1992), both of which involved several passes of the same roll through the camera with different frames exposed each time (both are sound films, too). This repeated passing of the roll through the camera also characterizes her *Bouquets*, but the main difference when she came to make the later series was that she was no longer weaving together images that were identically framed. The *Bouquets* intermingle shots of different places within the same general area, rather than comprising shots of exactly the same place at different times (there are also occasional frames that are shot normally and some blank frames). More freely than in *Rue des Teinturiers*, the filmed subjects construct the space that ordinary perception from the same standpoint could not ever achieve simultaneously, and an imagined space formed through intricate perceptual observation emerges through the layered images on the basis of Lowder's constantly shifting and creative engagement with the environments she films.

With the exception of *Bouquets* 6 and 8 in the first series, which do not feature any flora, flowers return persistently within the perceptual field. In *Bouquet* 1, for example, filmed at Mont Ventoux in Provence, in which shots from the base of the mountain intermingle with shots at the summit where people could buy sweets among other things, running water appears over flowers, as do landscapes over water, and flowers over cars and people. In *Bouquet* 13, filmed on an organic farm and agro-ecological site in Aujac in the Gard, shots of a butterfly and other insects, along with vegetables, intermesh with people working on the land, interspersed with and overlaid by flowers. Animals make regular appearances throughout the series, for example a cat and then a donkey in *Bouquet* 21 (Figure 1), filmed at the same farm in Aujac in the Gard through a haze of yellow flowers, in which farm workers and visitors also interweave throughout. And *Bouquet* 22, filmed in the pastures of the mountainous Grand Perron des Encombres, features images of the snow-streaked peaks, of buildings, of a children's play area, of people young and old, all of which mesh with the flowers (Figure 2). Human dominion is challenged as relationships with other forms of life — flowers most notably — come to the fore in a practice where visual perception frequently meets its limits.

To recall the equality and symmetry of measure that allowed me to link Scarry's association of beauty and the just to the perceptual–imaginative space of Lowder's early films by means of the philosophers' cube, it is the balance that Lowder achieves between the different aspects of her *Bouquets* that is important here, making people part of the picture alongside myriad other forms of life. The flowers assert their shimmering beauty, de-centring the human and thereby making people a less pivotal aspect of the filmed environments that viewers perceive. In this, Lowder's work is in tune with other philosophers who travel more explicitly the route that Scarry is interested in mapping from beauty to being just. Indeed, for moral philosopher Iris Murdoch, the experience of beauty involves an experience of 'unselfing' that links perception to a sense of justice. For Murdoch, experiencing beauty in the enjoyment of nature and art, as well as in intellectual disciplines, prompts an ability 'to forget self, to be realistic, to perceive justly'.[35] The beauty of nature that prompts perceiving justly involves imagining, too, as Murdoch affirms: 'We use our imagination not to escape the world but to join it.'[36] Murdoch's example as she introduces the experience of unselfing is a scene from nature. She describes looking out of the window one day and seeing a kestrel, a sight which distracted her from brooding thoughts and cleared her mind of selfish care to the point that she declares '[t]here is nothing now but kestrel'.[37] Building upon this example, she includes in the experience of unselfing 'delight in flowers';[38] and taking her observations into the realm of art, she talks of its genesis and enjoyment as 'a thing totally opposed to selfish obsession'.[39] Looking out of the window at a kestrel or taking delight in flowers may be close to the activity of the filmmaker who first scopes out her subjects in the environment prior to filming, but they are clearly different perceptual experiences from watching one of Lowder's films, in which the effect on natural perception of the apparatus is part of a broader experience.[40] Yet through the perceptual-imaginative space of her films Lowder reconnects creatively with a world that has the human in it but is not dominated by it. She is thus attuned to the work of unselfing that involves perceiving justly, and she attunes viewers of the *Bouquets* to this, too.

The fairness that pointed to loveliness of aspect as well as justice for Scarry in the journey that began with beauty joins here not only with her sense of perceptual acuity but also with the retraining of perception noted by MacDonald with reference to ecocinema and with the alteration of perception that Irigaray calls for in her ecophilosophy.

Fairness has an additional sense pertinent to this discussion, though, having stood historically as a marker of the female and the feminine. The sexual and gendered resonance of this term has long aided cultural associations between beauty, women and flowers to be passed off as natural and has placed a frequent barrier between women and the sense of fairness that is connected with justice.[41] Wherever reference to Mother Nature has served to essentialize the relationship between nature and the maternal-feminine, the feminine risks being eclipsed in culture, and while her survival in the latter domain is crucial, the networks of relations built beyond human reproduction are just as important. Lowder's work relates to the replication of beauty that Scarry talks about, but by remaining with and foregrounding the flowers, she sets herself apart from the sole replication of human beauty by means of reproduction. Lowder's enmeshing of different species in the environments she films may not have the stridency of feminist theorist Donna Haraway's call to 'Make Kin Not Babies', but her work has tacit affinities with this feminist ecological drive.[42] As Irigaray notes, the Western tradition has focused too much on the fruits rather than the flowers, on the bearing of the fruits of carnal love rather than the flowering of lovers.[43] For Lowder, to linger on the flowers while also bringing in other occupants of the ecological sites she films is to reach beyond the fruits of human relationships alone, and to make kin of all kinds. The symmetry of relations or balance between different forms of life is not about making everyone or everything like everything else but is, as Irigaray notes, vital to coexisting in difference, the first dwelling for which, when humans relate to the vegetal world, is the silence of a wordless encounter.[44]

Lowder's commitment to filming in 16mm in silence in these films — even though a function of much experimental filmmaking that has no explicit ecological connection — ensures nonetheless that the *Bouquets* correspond with such vegetal silence. Irigaray observes that, in the Western tradition, silence has been left to nature and to women assimilated to nature, and she seeks to reinvest it with a positive value while undoing the essentialist assimilation of women to nature.[45] Like Merleau-Ponty, Irigaray is interested in looking beyond what is visible to the eye, and while she follows him into invisible spaces, she has always paid more attention to the darkness of the starting point in life — initial contact with a mother's body in utero through touch and hearing — carrying this forwards and never forgetting this founding relation. For Irigaray in her earlier work the very operation necessary to bring the maternal-feminine into language 'requires passage through

Figure 1. *Bouquet* 21 (Rose Lowder, *Bouquets 21-30*, 2001-2005).

Figure 2. *Bouquet* 22 (Rose Lowder, *Bouquets 21-30*, 2002-2005).

the night, a light that remains in obscurity',[46] and she notes the importance of the voice for introducing sexuate difference. Lowder's *Bouquets* may not engage this vocal connection but they do embed the presence of the director's name and film title in fragmented form at the start of each bouquet of images, establishing a tacit connection to the female filmmaker, while involving her in the transformed world of her films, the letters of 'BOUQUETS' and of the proper name 'ROSE', also a flower, broken up and strewn like petals among the imaged flowers at the beginning or end of each film. Moreover, as a result of their seasonal unity, Lowder's films exude intense warmth and are flooded with light. The darkness into which one needs to venture, following Irigaray, thus seems initially to bear a less literal relation to Lowder's films than the silence. But attention to what cannot be perceived in the light is crucial to appreciate the life of plants, which grow above and below ground, and wherever there is a point of acknowledgment of obscurity in Lowder's *Bouquets*, viewers come into contact with this too. The flicker within the brightness of the films introduces this at regular intervals: the *photo* encounters the *phyto* between light and darkness — a condition of film, of course, but also the possibility of meeting flowers on their own terms. The connection to perceptual–imaginative space that I have been concerned with throughout serves this purpose too.

Indeed, thinking about an encounter with this obscurity in terms of an experience of what is never normally perceived from a given perspective — the experience of perceiving-imagining the entirety of the cube from one vantage point — the abiding importance of that initial figuration of perceptual–imaginative space can be invested now with a link to coexisting in difference. Lowder's ecologies constitute a way of being with the vegetal embedded in how she films her *Bouquets*, still in tune with Scarry's interest in fairness (loveliness of aspect/equality and symmetry of measure) that connected beauty to the just, but now bringing with it a de-essentialized link to the feminine, too. Lowder's exquisitely woven images are a privileged artistic site in which the concerns of aesthetics and moral philosophy meet those of ecophilosophy, with everything stemming from flowers in their habitat. Her ever-burgeoning *Bouquets* give rise to a distinctive encounter with the beauty of each individual film, which is never *juste un bouquet* but *un bouquet juste*.

NOTES

1   Rose Lowder, *Rose by Rose Lowder* (Paris: Light Cone Editions, 2015), 86.

2   After completing 1–10, Lowder began 11–20 but was not satisfied with them so made 21–30, which she ended up completing first, hence their non-chronological order (*Rose by Rose Lowder*, 83). In a Master Class at Lux, London in September 2018 she said that she is still making *Bouquets*.

3   See her DVD Interview (2002) on 'Cinéxperimentaux 5: Rose Lowder' (Re: Voir, 2014).

4   William English, 'Three Aspects of French Experiment: Interviews with Yann Beauvais and Rose Lowder and Alain-Alcide Sudre', *Millennium Film Journal* 23/24 (Winter 1990–1), 106–15.

5   Rose Lowder, 'Le Film expérimental en tant qu'instrument de recherche visuelle: contribution des cinéastes expérimentaux à une démarche exploratoire', 622, Light Cone archive, Paris.

6   Rose Lowder, 'The Filming and the Film: A Brief Introduction to the Work', March 1985, *Cantrills Filmnotes* 47/48 (August 1985), 56–60 (59).

7   P. Adams Sitney, *Visionary Film: The American Avant-Garde, 1943–2000*, 3rd edition (Oxford: Oxford University Press, 2002 [1974]), 347–70.

8   Rose Lowder, 'Leaving the Artist's Studio Behind or How to Make Bouquets Out of Flowers and Film', *Cantrills Filmnotes* 85/86 (June 1997), 54–8 (55).

9   Lowder, 'Le Film expérimental', 205.

10 The volume *Perception: Mechanisms and Models* (San Francisco: W. H. Freeman and Company, 1972), edited by Richard Held and Whitman Richards, is a recurrent reference point.

11 Jean-Paul Sartre, *The Imaginary: A Phenomenological Psychology of the Imagination*, translated by Jonathan Webber (London: Routledge, 2010 [1940]), 9 and Maurice Merleau-Ponty, *Phenomenology of Perception*, translated by Colin Smith (London: Routledge, 2002 [1945]), 235–39 and 306–8.

12 Sartre, *The Imaginary*, 8.

13 Merleau-Ponty, *Phenomenology of Perception*, 236.

14 My exploration of imagination here differs therefore from the focus of my earlier *Film and the Imagined Image* (Edinburgh: Edinburgh University Press, 2019), which was devoted to how spectators conjure vivid mental images while watching film.

15 Maurice Merleau-Ponty, 'Eye and Mind' in *The Merleau-Ponty Aesthetics Reader: Philosophy and Painting*, edited by Galen A. Johnson (Evanston: Northwestern University Press, 1993 [1960]), 121–49 (146). Initially close to Sartre in *Phenomenology of Perception* when writing about perception and imagination, Merleau-Ponty distances himself in his later work on imagination from his fellow phenomenologist. For more on this in relation to film, see Sarah Cooper, 'Merleau-Ponty and Film: Documenting the

Imagination' in *Understanding Merleau-Ponty, Understanding Modernism*, edited by Ariane Mildenberg (New York: Bloomsbury, 2019), 157–69.

16 Joseph Addison, *Essays on the Pleasures of the Imagination* (Antwerp: Duverger & Co., 1828), 7. His essays appeared originally in *The Spectator* in 1712.

17 Addison, *Pleasures*, 3.

18 Immanuel Kant, *Observations on the Feeling of the Beautiful and Sublime and Other Writings*, edited and translated Patrick Frierson and Paul Guyer (Cambridge: Cambridge University Press, 2011 [1764]), 14.

19 Immanuel Kant, *Critique of Judgment*, translated by Werner S. Pluhar (Indianapolis: Hackett Publishing Company, 1987 [1790]), 114.

20 Kant, *Critique of Judgment*, 112–13.

21 Kant, *Critique of Judgment*, 115.

22 Kant, *Critique of Judgment*, 115.

23 Elaine Scarry, *On Beauty and Being Just* (Princeton: Princeton University Press, 1999), 84.

24 When Scarry addresses imaginability elsewhere, the size of the object to be imagined is important. Flowers are exemplary objects for her: their size, shape and localization, as well as the rarity of their petals, lend themselves to vivid imagining. See her *Dreaming by the Book* (Princeton: Princeton University Press, 2001 [1999]), 40–71.

25 Guinevere Narraway, 'Strange Seeing: Re-viewing Nature in the Films of Rose Lowder' in *Screening Nature: Cinema Beyond the Human*, edited by Anat Pick and Guinevere Narraway (Oxford: Berghahn, 2013), 213–24 (221).

26 Scarry, *On Beauty and Being Just*, 51. For a critique of the denigration of the pretty specific to film, see Rosalind Galt, *Pretty: Film and the Decorative Image* (New York: Columbia University Press, 2011).

27 Scarry, *On Beauty and Being Just*, 94.

28 Scarry, *On Beauty and Being Just*, 3–6.

29 Enrico Camporesi, 'A Filmic Exploration by Means of Botanical Imagery: Notes on Rose Lowder', *NECSUS*, Spring 2013, https://necsus-ejms.org/a-filmic-exploration-by-means-of-botanical-imagery-notes-on-rose-lowder/, consulted 21 January 2019.

30 Lowder, DVD Interview (2002).

31 Scarry, *On Beauty and Being Just*, 88.

32 Scarry, *On Beauty and Being Just*, 61.

33 Scott MacDonald, 'Toward an Eco-Cinema', *ISLE* 11:2 (July 2004), 107–32 (109); Narraway, 'Strange Seeing', 221.

34 Luce Irigaray and Michael Marder, *Through Vegetal Being: Two Philosophical Perspectives* (New York: Columbia University Press, 2016), 48.

35 Iris Murdoch, 'The Sovereignty of Good over Other Concepts' in *The Sovereignty of Good* (London: Routledge, 2014 [1970]), 75–100 (88).

36 Murdoch, 'The Sovereignty', 88.

37 Murdoch, 'The Sovereignty', 82.
38 Murdoch, 'The Sovereignty', 82.
39 Murdoch, 'The Sovereignty', 83.
40 For an exploration of Murdoch's 'unselfing' in relation to film as an art form, see Lucy Bolton, *Contemporary Cinema and the Philosophy of Iris Murdoch* (Edinburgh: Edinburgh University Press, 2019).
41 Scarry's sense of fairness is centred on loveliness of aspect but there is a far more pernicious association with fairness in Edmund Burke's work on beauty and the sublime. Burke describes colours of beautiful bodies as 'clean and fair' not 'dusky and muddy' initiating a hierarchy in skin colour that links to race and then blackness as the text progresses. See Edmund Burke, *A Philosophical Inquiry into the Origin of our Ideas of the Sublime and Beautiful* (London: Howlett and Brimmer, 1823 [1757]), 169. For more on the question of race in Burke's and Kant's theories, see Meg Armstrong, '"The Effects of Blackness": Gender, Race, and the Sublime in the Aesthetic Theories of Burke and Kant', *The Journal of Aesthetics and Art Criticism* 54:3 (Summer 1996), 213–36.
42 Haraway's slogan appears throughout *Staying with the Trouble: Making Kin in the Chthulucene* (Durham, NC: Duke University Press, 2016).
43 Irigaray, in Irigaray and Marder, *Through Vegetal Being*, 38.
44 Irigaray, in Irigaray and Marder, *Through Vegetal Being*, 50.
45 Irigaray, in Irigaray and Marder, *Through Vegetal Being*, 49–50.
46 Luce Irigaray, 'The Invisible of the Flesh: A Reading of Merleau-Ponty, *The Visible and the Invisible*, "The Intertwining — The Chiasm"' in *An Ethics of Sexual Difference*, translated by Carolyn Burke and Gillian C. Gill (Ithaca: Cornell University Press, 1993 [1984]), 151–84 (152).

'The Cruel Radiance of What Is': Empathy, Imagination and Estrangement in Johan van der Keuken's *Face Value* and *Herman Slobbe*

ABRAHAM GEIL

In an enigmatic late text the German filmmaker and theorist Harun Farocki revisited the question of empathy, a term which he had long dismissed as belonging to 'the other side'.[1] Empathy was aligned with the Aristotelean notion of catharsis and its modern derivations of emotional identification in bourgeois theatre and commercial cinema. It belonged to that entire domain of aesthetic experience that Brecht's famous *Verfremdungseffekt* targeted for disruption.[2] Farocki's interest in empathy in this 2008 text, entitled simply *Einfühlung*, should not, however, be taken as a late-life renunciation of his Brechtian commitments. Rather, he poses the possibility for a radical rethinking of the category of empathy itself, which, he says, 'is too good a word to leave to any other side'.[3] Farocki's question, then, is how to think empathy differently so as to wrest it from the hands of the enemy. He concludes his text with a kind of provocation: 'It should be possible to empathize in such a way that it produces the effect of estrangement.'[4]

That is the possibility this article aims to explore vis-à-vis the question of film and imagination. I take up Farocki's provocation to suggest a vantage for rethinking the recent polemics around empathy — both its valorization in the liberal common sense of Euro-American public culture as an essential moral attribute and social cure-all as well as its critique in contemporary strains of critical theory. What empathy's proponents and its critics tend to share is a notion of empathy as an ideal of intersubjective transparency. The facile erasure of difference for which it is rightly critiqued depends upon a presumed relation of immediacy: as an 'imagined image' of another, empathy is

Paragraph 43.3 (2020): 330–347
DOI: 10.3366/para.2020.0344
© Edinburgh University Press
www.euppublishing.com/para

thought to transform concrete images into vanishing mediators in the service of moral imagination. The question, following Farocki's lead, is how to conceptualize a relation of imagination and the filmic image that would sustain the apparent oxymoron of empathic estrangement.

If there is a privileged site for the imagination of empathy in film and its afterlives, it is surely the image of the human face. The face marks the 'scene of empathy' in which cognitive film theorists most notably have found the moral imaginations of spectators at work.[5] Rather than adopting a pre-given notion of empathy to illuminate the relation between film and the spectator's moral imagination, I want to ask how film — and the use of facial images specifically — can force us to rethink the conception of empathy itself. This means approaching empathy and moral imagination as a problem of form in the first instance rather than a question of psychological experience. That is, instead of considering how a particular image of the face may or may not solicit what we could call an act of empathic imagination, the task is to ask how that imagination is constituted in and through the form of the image to begin with. The image of the face then becomes a kind of imaginary terrain in which to explore very different notions of what might count as empathy.

Before proceeding further let me briefly sketch some of the major positions and fault lines that run through contemporary debates over empathy. Proponents of empathy tend to describe it as a rapidly diminishing capacity or resource. In *The Audacity of Hope* (2006), for example, Barack Obama famously diagnosed US culture as suffering from an 'empathy deficit'.[6] More recently, in *Zero Degrees of Empathy* (2011), the British neuro-psychologist Simon Baron-Cohen has cast the problem on a transnational stage, warning that the 'erosion of empathy is an important global issue related to the health of our communities, be they small (like families) or big (like nations)'.[7] Meanwhile, developments in neuroscience around so-called 'mirror neurons' that purport to find a neurobiological, evolutionarily grounded basis for empathy have led other commentators to take a more optimistic view. The most grandiose example is no doubt Jeremy Rifkin's 2009 tome *The Empathic Civilization*. Rifkin begins by announcing that 'A radical new view of human nature is emerging in the biological and cognitive sciences (. . .) The dawning realization that we are a fundamentally empathic species has profound and far-reaching consequences for society.'[8] This innate fact of human nature, however, must not only be discovered but also achieved as the culmination of world civilization. Thus, for Rifkin, '[t]he most important question facing humanity is this: Can we reach *global empathy* in time to avoid the collapse of civilization and save the Earth?'[9] Hyperbole aside, this last statement expresses two essential hallmarks of the redemptive image of empathy: first, that it is a natural capacity on the order of what was once called a 'moral instinct' and that, therefore, it is not fundamentally a matter of social production but rather of empathy's rediscovery at the heart of human nature and its subsequent reanimation in the social. The second, related hallmark, is that empathy as a social good will seamlessly *scale* between the levels of the interpersonal, the social and indeed the global. I will return to these two features below to describe how empathy has been recruited in Euro-American political thought as an imaginary supplement for a Rousseau-inspired politics of recognition.

For critics of the positive view of empathy sketched above, the core scenario of intersubjective reciprocity upon which it is based is a pernicious illusion. That is, rather than enabling one to genuinely occupy the position of another, empathy is nothing more than a narcissistic projection of self onto other. On this view, empathy erases difference and occludes structural inequality for the sake of a cheap, self-congratulatory expiation of guilt in the face of suffering and bare life. Saidiya Hartman has provided one of most trenchant critiques of empathy along these lines with her argument that when the spectacle of Black suffering is taken as an occasion for white empathy that suffering is effectively reinscribed into a property relation which has its historical foundation in chattel slavery.[10] Empathy is the master's prerogative: to do whatever he wishes with the Black body, including projecting himself into it.[11] Other critics have focused on the way empathy has become a kind of Silicon Valley trope that obscures a generalized dismantling of political agency. In this recourse to empathy, as Jan Slaby puts it, 'the *de facto* powerlessness of the individual in today's network capitalism is naturalized through a model of "visceral sociality" that prizes affective attachment and harmonious connectedness'.[12]

To be clear, I find these lines of critique powerful and persuasive with respect to the prevailing common sense about empathy. My aim in this article is to consider how this common sense is not just presumed in a certain understanding of the relation between the spectatorial imagination and the image but gets constituted in and through specific uses of the image of the face. In the instances I consider here, I argue, the empathic imagination depends upon the facial image as an aesthetic supplement. This approach opens the possibility of thinking the operation of the empathic imagination otherwise, in the spirit of Farocki's provocation, by taking it up from the side of the image — not as a vanishing mediator at the service of the imagination but rather as an estranging form that calls it persistently into question.

Einfühlung *Aesthetics from Experience to Form*

My first step in thinking an image of empathy as estrangement is genealogical: to estrange the concept of empathy itself by sketching the history of its constitution prior to the contemporary usage. It was not until shortly after the Second World War that empathy began to circulate in popular discourse as a term describing interpersonal relations.[13] As is well known, the concept originated in late nineteenth-century German aesthetics in the term *Einfühlung* — literally 'feeling into' — before migrating into early twentieth-century experimental psychology and subsequently being translated in the Anglo-American context as empathy. The word *Einfühlung* was first codified as a technical term in aesthetics by the German philosopher of art Robert Vischer in 1873 to describe how observers project meaning onto spatial form. It was adopted by the German philosopher and psychologist Theodor Lipps at the turn of the twentieth century and broadened to encompass the experience not only of aesthetic objects but also the mental states of other people through an instinctual process of inner imitation. The precise depiction of that process was never entirely fixed: 'projection, transfer, association, animation, personification, vivification, fusion, identification' were among the possibilities considered.[14]

'Empathy' was coined around 1909 by the psychologists James Ward at Cambridge and Edward Titchener at Cornell. Taken from the Greek, it was chosen as a technical term to distinguish itself from the popular term 'sympathy'. Importantly, Titchener insisted (against Lipps) that empathy was not an adequate way to understand the thoughts and feelings of others. Whereas now, in a curious historical reversal in meaning, the erosion of empathy is understood to result in taking other subjects *as* objects, according to Titchener the ontological difference between the subject and its object was the very precondition of empathy.

The aesthetic object whose birth coincided with the final period of *Einfühlung*'s prestige as both an aesthetic and psychological concept was, of course, cinema. This fact has not been lost upon film scholars, especially Germanists, among whom there has been a recent upsurge of interest in *Einfühlung* aesthetics. Scott Curtis, for example, situates *Einfühlung* in relation to the various cultural panics in Germany provoked by early cinema, and he argues that *Einfühlung* aesthetics can be seen as an attempt to reconcile the embodied experience of mass reception with an aesthetic ideology centred on individual contemplation.[15] In this role as an ideological mediator, we can see a prefiguration of the way empathy is now taken to scale between the moral imagination of the individual and the political imaginary of the collective.

Where my approach departs from this extremely fruitful line of historical work on *Einfühlung* is that I am less interested in recovering its original conception and scene of reception.[16] In Robin Curtis's gloss, Lipps understands *Einfühlung* to describe the process whereby we perceive 'in the form of things (. . .) an analogy to the expressive quality of the vitality of the human body' which we experience through 'an involuntary, instinctive mimicry' that results in an 'automatic form of sympathetic experience'.[17] Although Lipps sees *Einfühlung* as being based on a kind of projection, it is essential for him that we do not *experience* it as such. Rather, we feel our own vitality animated *in* the object. Hence Lipps's famous thesis that aesthetic enjoyment is in fact 'objectified self-enjoyment'. It is difficult to see where a moment of estrangement or simple distance could enter into this picture of a closed loop in which form — whether of an art object, a film or a person — is fundamentally understood as an occasion to experience the vitality of your own aesthetic and moral imagination resonating back to you.

Indeed, if one of the crucial insights offered by tracing the genealogy of *Einfühlung* is that empathy was an aesthetic concept before it was a moral one, it is necessary to consider the specific aesthetic tradition *Einfühlung* belongs to — not for the sake of policing fidelity to that tradition, but rather, for our purposes, to ask how we might *extract* it from that tradition and win it for another. *Einfühlung* aesthetics was situated squarely within early twentieth-century debates about the nature of the aesthetic experience that followed along a dominant line in German aesthetics since Kant wherein, as Scott Curtis puts it, 'the question of value hinged on *reception* more than form'.[18] That is, '[t]he value and legitimacy of art in this system depended primarily on the singularity of the experience it aroused'.[19] This system thus stood in distinction from the Hegelian tradition, 'which was concerned with how meaning inhered in form rather than how we experienced it'.[20]

Simply put, what I am proposing is to think empathy from that latter perspective: rather than approaching it through the category of experience, I want to take empathy up from the side of form. This entails shifting from a broadly phenomenological perspective of empathy that asks how objects or other subjects appear from the inside, so to speak, of a spectator's imagination to something more like a dramaturgical perspective that asks how scenes of empathy are staged in concrete images. Here I have in mind something close to what Jacques Rancière means when he describes a 'scene' as 'a little optical machine', not for illustrating concepts but rather for capturing 'concepts at work' by showing how thought weaves 'together perceptions, affects, names and ideas' in constituting the very conditions by which a concept becomes 'thinkable' to begin with.[21]

If our concept in question is the empathic imagination, by which we mean something like the process whereby an imagined image of another is produced, it is then a matter of examining how particular scenes or arrangements of images constitute that process along potentially very different lines. In the following section, I want to consider one staging of what we might call the dominant 'liberal' understanding of the empathic imagination, an online video produced by Amnesty International that uses images of the human face as vanishing mediators for achieving an effect of unmediated understanding and reciprocity between European subjects and refugees from Syria and Somalia. My subsequent reading of Johan van der Keuken's *Face Value* (1991) and *Herman Slobbe* (1966) aims to elucidate a counterimage of that dominant understanding of the empathic imagination, specifically in its use of facial images to operate the transition from an intersubjective scene to a broader political imaginary.

Empathic Imagination as Political Imaginary

When Charles Taylor, in his influential essay 'The Politics of Recognition' (1992), needs a scene for his ideal 'regime of reciprocal recognition among equals',[22] he turns not to Hegel's famous struggle unto death in the 'Lordship and Bondage' section of the *Phenomenology of Spirit* but to Jean-Jacques Rousseau's critique of the theatre in *Letter to D'Alembert*. Against theatre's separation of actor and spectator,

Rousseau praises the mutuality epitomized in the Republican festival held outdoors. Here is the passage Taylor appropriates for his image of late-twentieth-century reciprocity:

Plant a stake crowned with flowers in the middle of a square; gather the people together there, and you will have a festival. (...) let the spectators become an entertainment to themselves; make them actors themselves; do it so that each sees and loves himself in the others so that all will be better united.[23]

Critics have long noted the paradoxically theatrical element in Rousseau's attempts to figure equality as a natural instinct.[24] He must, in effect, *stage* the abolishment of theatre through the vanishing mediator of the maypole, which figures a circular movement of perpetually exchanged positions against the fixed hierarchical separation of the elevated stage. What Rousseau stages here is an imaginary of the collective in a scene of intersubjectivity — a social theory of the mirror.

With Rousseau's maypole dance in mind — or, rather, Taylor's recruitment of that image for a politics of recognition in the 1990s — I want to leap to the contemporary moment in which the sociopolitical imaginary of Europe articulated in that earlier, post-1989 moment has experienced profound stress fractures under the pressure of the so-called 'refugee crisis' around 2015 and the turn to right-wing nationalism that has sought to exploit it. Specifically, I want to consider an attempt to deploy empathic imagination as an intervention in that crisis at the level of public sentiment: a video entitled '#Look Beyond Borders', which was produced in 2016 by Amnesty International Poland together with the advertising agency DDB & Tribal.[25] Framed as an 'experiment' inspired by the much-publicized work on love by the social psychologist Arthur Aron, this video is set in a converted warehouse in Berlin located near Checkpoint Charlie for its symbolic value. Refugees from Syria and Somalia are placed opposite volunteers from Belgium, Italy, Germany, Poland and the UK (who are presumably proxies for the intended European audience of the video). They are then, according to the conceit of the experiment, filmed as they stare into each other's eyes for four minutes, which, according to Aron's research, will involuntarily induce feelings of intimate mutuality (Figure 1).

No doubt this video partakes in an increasingly recognizable genre: the humanitarian variation upon a now-familiar nexus between the converted warehouse *mise en scène* of contemporary soap commercials and TED Talk-style social psychology packaged, in a bid for viral

Mariam, Syria

Lee, UK

Figure 1. *Look Beyond Borders* (Amnesty International, 2016).

circulation, under a hashtag slogan.[26] What I am specifically interested in here, however, is the way in which this video operates formally as something like a twenty-first-century update of Rousseau's maypole dance *à la* Charles Taylor — a *dispositif* through which 'each sees and loves himself in the others so that all will be better united'. Like the maypole dance, the '#Look Beyond Borders' video stages a scene of empathic imagination through an arrangement of elements that aims to erase the division between spectator and spectacle. In this case, that means overcoming the separation between subjects whose positions are essentially asymmetrical — the figure of the European citizen and the figure of the refugee — by staging the horizontal vector of face-to-face eye contact.[27] The rhetorical framing of the video as an 'experiment' makes this staging explicit as its subjects become the spectacle for us as quasi-scientific investigators. At the same time, the promotional material invites us to 'look refugees in the eye'. Thus, the spectator is not left solely in the position of third-person observer but has their empathic imagination directly solicited by being sutured into the 'experiment' as a pseudo participant through the classical film grammar of shot/reverse shot.

Draginja Nadaždin, the director of Amnesty International Poland, proclaims: 'It takes a heart of stone to watch this video without shedding a tear. Today, when the world appears rife with division and conflict, it is always worthwhile to look at everything from another person's perspective.' But if some notion of empathy as perspective-taking is clearly being invoked here, what precisely is the logic of empathic imagination staged in the video's conceit of an 'experimental' scene? In the first place, the video presents a series of immediate encounters in which two people are put into a relation of intersubjective presence without the mediation of language or common culture. The work of empathic imagination thus staged here involves what we might call a pedagogy of anamnesis. Naturalized as a moral instinct — an immediate, pre-reflective capacity — empathy cannot be learned; it can only be, as it were, unforgotten, recovered or rather uncovered from beneath the ossifications of culture. The image of the face is the aesthetic supplement that enables this conception of the empathic imagination as the conduit between the interpersonal and the collective to go through.[28] On the one hand, the facial image is the vanishing mediator for the empathic imagination of others as a process of unmediated reciprocity. On the other, the image of the face returns, as it were, *qua* image to be taken up by this imagination to perform a double function: it becomes at once the sensible homology for the cohesion of an organic social totality and the site where that cohesion is supposed to take hold experientially.

Empathic Estrangement in Face Value *and* Herman Slobbe

Appearing as it did during the post-1989 moment in which the political consensus around a politics of recognition was forming in Western Europe as well as North America, it would be all too tempting to assimilate Van der Keuken's 1991 *Face Value* into that consensus. What better demonstration of the empathic imagination's capacity to scale from the intersubjective to the socio-political imaginary that I sketch above with respect to the '#Look Beyond Borders' video than a film that composes a collective portrait of Europe almost entirely out of close-ups of faces?[29] But my argument in what follows is that, if *Face Value* speaks to a (naturalized) notion of empathic imagination which subtends the consensual politics of mutual recognition in the imaginary of Europe emerging at that moment, it is in order to take it as a problem to struggle with and against at a formal level. Here is Van der Keuken's own description of the film:

You can see the film as a compilation of very different positions and places that people occupy, in a field of relations. And that field of relations you might call Europe, an incomplete Europe, that perhaps only exists in the imagination, between London, Marseille, Prague, Germany and the Netherlands. *Face Value* revolves around the face and seeing: the desire to be seen, the fear of being seen, the impossibility of seeing oneself, the fear and the desire to see others.[30]

How then are we to understand this incomplete Europe of the imagination which consists of a 'field of relations' rendered visible almost exclusively through images of faces? One possible approach would be to describe this project in terms of an 'aesthetics of cognitive mapping', which Fredric Jameson was conceptualizing around the same time.[31] Certainly, this concept would appear perfectly consequent with another one of Van der Keuken's late films, *Amsterdam Global Village* (1996), which uses the device of a young Moroccan courier delivering photographs on a scooter to clients all over Amsterdam to produce a kind of cognitive map of the city. Unlike that later film, however, *Face Value* rigorously eschews any attempt to directly trace a social totality.

It is the great French film critic Serge Daney who gets us closer, I think, in an essay he wrote about the filmmaker for *Cahiers du cinéma* in 1978. Daney borrows his striking title for this essay, 'The Cruel Radiance of What Is', from a passage in James Agee and Walker Evans's *Let Us Now Praise Famous Men* (1941). Although Daney is addressing an earlier phase of Van der Keuken's work, the essay nevertheless sheds a proleptic light on precisely the aspects of *Face Value* I wish to explore here. Daney begins with the following claim:

There are, properly speaking, no scenes in the films of JVdK, but *fragments*. Not parts of all that is to come and certainly not the pieces of a puzzle to reconstruct. But fragments of *cinema*. (. . .) [I]t's the fragment that fixes our look, appropriates it and, in turn, looks at us. Cut off from everything, the fragment of cinema gives us the eye.[32]

This could be a description of *Face Value* itself: the film as an assemblage of fragment-faces, each gazing implacably back at the viewer, together refusing to coalesce into a single overall picture. The fragment, Daney continues, 'is affected by two possible futures: fetishistic and dialectical'.[33] These two 'futures' can be understood as the poles that constitute the terrain upon which *Face Value* plays out. In its fate as fetish, the face-fragment would assume the status of its own self-sufficient totality. But what then of the 'field of relations' Van der Keuken invokes in his description of the film, the 'positions and places' from which these fragments, as Daney puts it, 'give us the eye'? The dialectical fate of the face-fragment poses the opposite problem as its singularity is subsumed into the totality. We have already seen one kind of solution to this problem through the empathic imagination staged in the face-to-face topos of the '#Look Beyond Borders' video, which elevates the face itself into the site where these two poles are reconciled. Van der Keuken's task in *Face Value* is, to the contrary, precisely not to reconcile the fetishistic and dialectical 'futures' of the face-fragment but rather to sustain their tension through what Daney describes as a violent oscillation.

There is no single formal operation at the heart of *Face Value* but rather a diverse collection all of which can nevertheless loosely fit within the genre of the portrait. Certainly, it would be possible to situate this tendency as a kind of extension and reworking of the tradition of classical Dutch painting. But as if to pre-empt such a reading, *Face Value* begins with a scene of children dressed in the clichéd costumes of the Dutch Golden Age and posing for photographs in front of anachronistically painted backgrounds. At the same time, there is an immediate displacement when one realizes that the photographer is speaking Czech and that this photoshoot of clichéd Dutch poses is likely happening in Prague. In this instance and many others, the oscillation between the fetishistic and the dialectical 'fate' of the face fragment is internal to the film's individual portraits.

With this notion of internal disjunction in mind, I want to look at one of the portrait set-ups that recurs, with variations, throughout *Face Value*: a subject is shot in close-up — sometimes engaged in work, sometimes simply staring at the camera — while we hear an off-screen voice, presumably belonging to the same subject and recorded at a different time, as they narrate some aspect of their experience (Figure 2). Thus, crucially, these are sound as much as optical portraits, the audio captured and mixed by Van der Keuken's long-time collaborator Noshka van der Lely. Because there are no establishing shots, with the film often cutting straight to another close-up of a face in some other country, it is typically the national language of the voice that enables us to orient ourselves geographically.

Somehow I'm the captain girl
of the group.

I got out of it
because I had to choose.

Figure 2. *Face Value* (Johan van der Keuken, 1991).

What is the effect of this specific interplay between face and voice? Film theorists have long been intrigued by such instances in the history of film — close-ups of the face with an out-of-frame voiceover. For Michel Chion, for example, the voice makes the face into a kind of mask which, pushed to an extreme, creates an 'analogy between the surface of the skin and the material film surface'.[34] Conversely, in a view exemplified by Roland Barthes's lyrical descriptions of the 'grain of the voice' at the end of the *Pleasure of the Text*, the voice is thought to give the body back to the face, to *enflesh* it.[35] There is also the less often asked question of what the face does to the voice. Does the face's exteriority render the voice into a direct expression of interiority? Or does the face's spontaneous, unmediated expressivity expose the voice as hopelessly mired in the conventional mediation of serial signification?

The genius of a work like *Face Value* is to render all of these positions into just so many false choices. The voice-over does not reveal the interior or true self of the person hidden underneath the mask of the face, nor is the face an immediate revelation of the person behind the voice. Neither face nor voice is privileged; neither is the guarantor for the truth of the other. Rather, these optical/sound portraits in *Face Value* operate something closer to what Gilles Deleuze would call a 'disjunctive synthesis' out of which differences ramify across a series. Rather than functioning as just so many occasions for the imagination of the spectator to engage in an instance of empathic reciprocity (as I claimed is the case with '#Look Beyond Borders') the internal disjuncture of *Face Value*'s optical/sound portraits arguably produces an effect of distance that enables each to mark out a distinct position within what Van der Keuken calls 'a field of relations'.

This effect can be linked to what Thomas Elsaesser has brilliantly elucidated as 'an aesthetics of sensory asymmetry' that informs all of Van der Keuken's work.[36] Most concretely, Elsaesser associates this aesthetics with Van der Keuken's long-standing interest in making portraits of subjects with sensory disabilities. The first portrait in *Face Value* is in fact of an elderly man who has gone nearly blind and later two deaf children appear signing together. Van der Keuken seeks out these border situations, as Daney puts it, where 'there can be no "good place" for the filmmaker. The unequal exchange, if I dare say so, stares you in the face.'[37]

While *Face Value* was one of Van der Keuken's last films, I want to now conclude by turning to one of his first, *Herman Slobbe* (or *Blind Kind 2*), from 1966, in which the notions of 'sensory asymmetry' and 'unequal exchange' find a remarkable early expression. In 1964 Van der Keuken spent two months making a documentary entitled *Blind Kind/ Blind Child* at a residential institute for blind children in the Netherlands. He was intrigued by a certain child named Herman Slobbe and came back two years later to make a portrait film about him as a kind of sequel to the earlier documentary.

What do we make of the relation of sensory asymmetry entailed in the close-up of a blind person's face, which figures prominently in *Blind Kind 2*? A face for whom the other is not a face, or at least not the image of a face, but a voice or a touch? Empathy as a matter of simple perspective switching is profoundly complicated here. The reciprocity of vision figured in the face-to-face topos of the Amnesty International video is blocked by an apparent asymmetry. For Daney, this 'unequal exchange' is a 'scandal', but a 'precious' one:

Because it's on this condition that *Blind Kind 2* sends back to oblivion all that could have been — humanitarian documentary to shameful voyeurism — and ends up giving us access to the character of Herman Slobbe, as he also exists outside of the film, with his own projects, his callousness, and most of all — that's where the biggest scandal lies — his pleasure.[38]

Indeed, much of the film is devoted precisely to an exploration of Herman's pleasure as we follow him while he indulges in his various preoccupations, which include listening to Black American music, recording mock radio broadcasts, attending car races, and teasing his mother. In one sequence, he argues with his mother over his desire to watch a car race in person as opposed to seeing it on television.

Figure 3. *Herman Slobbe* (Johan van der Keuken,1966).

She tells him that it should not matter because in either case he will not be 'watching' it. Later, we see Herman at a car race and see footage and audio of the cars themselves careening around the track. But this sequence turns out to be deceptive as the film cuts, via a sound bridge, to reveal that it is Herman himself, sitting in his living room, who is producing the soundtrack of racing cars through a masterful manipulation of the microphone and his own mouth sounds. This sequence explicitly plays with the relation between image and audio tracks in a way that foregrounds an aesthetics of sensory asymmetry. Here the asymmetry is not between Van der Keuken's camera eye which sees what Herman cannot, but in the distinction created between two planes of sensory experience, the visual and aural, through their relations of slippage and alignment.

For all of that, the portrait of Herman feels in fact quite intimate, which makes the ending all the more shocking. Without warning, the film cuts to an entirely different landscape and Van der Keuken's voiceover announces: 'Now we drop Herman. I am going to Spain to shoot a new film.' Over a scene of labourers shot we can presume in Spain for this new film, Van de Keuken continues: 'Everything in a film is a form.' The film cuts back a final time to Herman as if to say goodbye. 'Herman is a form. See you later, sweet form' (Figure 3).

With this ending in mind I want to return to Farocki's provocation: 'It should be possible to empathize in such a way that it produces the effect of estrangement.' The effect of this abrupt ending whereby Herman is suddenly dispatched so that Van der Keuken can move on to his next project is not, I think, estrangement in the sense of unmasking the *true* relation between filmmaker and subject. What it shows is not simply the illusion or falsity of an empathic relation, as though having first drawn us into the hidden world of this obnoxious and adorable boy, having fooled us into believing we might know and care about this person, Van der Keuken then violently brings us into the truth that he was *using* Herman — and, by extension, the spectator — all along. That empathy, in other words, is but a ruse for the instrumentalization of the other and perhaps this truth is generalizable to the documentary relation as such. But that is clearly not the effect of the ending of *Blind Kind 2* any more than it is to stage an intersubjective scene of empathic imagination.

What is shown is both simpler and more elusive. On the one hand, it is a mere statement of fact, Herman *is* only a form, an object in the film like other objects. We should not confuse this object with the living breathing person Herman who has his own life — the scandal of his pleasure, as Daney puts it. On the other hand, however, *that* Herman has this existence outside of the film — that he exceeds the film and indeed that we can claim some access or relation to that excess — is only possible on the condition that *in* the film he is a form. This suggests a rather different interpretation of Titchener's insistence, which I note above, that the precondition of empathy is the ontological difference between subjects and objects. This would be a way of thinking how empathy could produce an effect of estrangement while nonetheless remaining, in some unfamiliar sense, empathy.

NOTES

1 Harun Farocki, 'Einfühlung/Empathy' [2008] in *Harun Farocki.: Another Kind of Empathy*, edited by Antje Ehmann and Carles Guerra (Barcelona: Fundación Antoni Tapies, 2016), 104. Originally published in *100 Jahre Hebbel Theater. Angewandtes Theaterlexikon nach Gustav Freiytag*, edited by Hebbel am Ufer (Berlin: primeline print, 2008), 21–2.

2 See, for example, Bertolt Brecht, 'Indirect Impact of the Epic Theatre (extracts from the Notes to *Die Mutter*)' in *Brecht on Theatre: The Development of an Aesthetic*, edited by John Willet (New York: Hill & Wang, 1992 [1933]), 57–62.

3 Farocki, 'Einfühlung/Empathy', 105.

4 Farocki, 'Einfühlung/Empathy', 105.

5 See, for example, Carl Plantinga, 'The Scene of Empathy and the Human Face on Film' in *Passionate Views: Film, Cognition, and Emotion*, edited by Carl Plantinga and Greg M. Smith (Baltimore: The Johns Hopkins University Press, 1999), and Alex Neill, 'Empathy and (Film) Fiction'

in *Post-Theory: Reconstructing Film Studies*, edited by David Bordwell and Noël Carroll (Madison: The University of Wisconsin Press, 1996).

6   Barack Obama, *The Audacity of Hope: Thoughts on Reclaiming the American Dream* (New York: Three Rivers Press, 2006), 67.

7   Simon Baron-Cohen, *Zero Degrees of Empathy: A New Theory of Human Cruelty* (London: Penguin, 2011), 124. I borrow this and the Obama example from Carolyn Pedwell's transformative critique of the transnational politics of empathy: 'Decolonising Empathy: Thinking Affect Transnationally', *Samyukta: A Journal of Women's Studies*, Special Issue, 'Decolonizing Theories of the Emotions', edited by S. Gunew, 16:1 (Jan 2016), 27–49.

8   Jeremy Rifkin, *The Empathic Civilization: The Race to Global Consciousness in a World in Crisis* (New York: Penguin Group, 2009), 1.

9   Rifkin, *The Empathic Civilization*, 3.

10 Saidiya V. Hartman, *Scenes of Subjection: Terror, Slavery, and Self-Making in Nineteenth-Century America* (Oxford: Oxford University Press, 1997).

11 Jordan Peele neatly captured the contemporary resonance of this dynamic in describing his film *Get Out* as a documentary, https://twitter.com/jordanpeele/status/930796561302540288?lang=en, consulted 18 October 2019.

12 Jan Slaby, 'Against Empathy: Critical Theory and the Social Brain', *Center for Building a Culture of Empathy*, http://cultureofempathy.com/References/Experts/Jan-Slaby.htm, consulted 18 October 2019.

13 Susan Lanzoni, *Empathy: A History* (New Haven: Yale University Press, 2018), 12.

14 Lanzoni, *Empathy*, 306. See also Andrea Pinotti, 'Empathy' in *Handbook of Phenomenological Aesthetics*, edited by Hans Rainer Sepp and Lester Embree (Dordrecht: Springer, 2010), 94.

15 Scott Curtis, *The Shape of Spectatorship: Art, Science, and Early Cinema in Germany* (New York: Columbia University Press, 2015), 193–241.

16 It should be noted that the interest of these scholars is not purely historical. By returning to the original scene of *Einfühlung*, Robin Curtis, for example, has sought resources for rethinking contemporary film and media concepts such as immersion. See Robin Curtis, 'Einfühlung and Abstraction in the Moving Image: Historical and Contemporary Reflections', *Science in Context* 25:3 (September 2012), 425–46.

17 Curtis, 'Einfühlung and Abstraction', 429.

18 Curtis, *The Shape of Spectatorship*, 195.

19 Curtis, *The Shape of Spectatorship*, 195.

20 Curtis, *The Shape of Spectatorship*, 195.

21 Jacques Rancière, *Aisthesis: Scenes from the Aesthetic Regime of Art*, translated by Zakir Paul (New York: Verso, 2013), xi. In addition to Rancière's general conception of a 'scene', I would identify two other more direct precedents for the approach to empathy I take here. The first, already mentioned above,

is the approach taken by Saidiya Hartman in her pathbreaking work *Scenes of Subjection* in which she elucidates the expropriative violence underlying white empathic projection by analysing the imaginative scenes played out upon what she calls 'the stage of sufferance' (17). The second, very different, precedent lies in the approach Susan Lanzoni takes in her magisterial study *Empathy: A History*, which is organized around 'nine historical stagings of different empathic practices over the past century' (15).

22   Charles Taylor, 'The Politics of Recognition' in *Multiculturalism: Examining the Politics of Recognition*, edited by Amy Gutmann (Princeton: Princeton University Press, 1994), 50.

23   Jean-Jacques Rousseau, *Politics and the Arts, Letter to M. d'Alembert on the Theatre* (Glencoe: Free Press, 1960), 126; quoted in Taylor, 'The Politics of Recognition', 47–8.

24   As David Marshall puts it: 'Rousseau's own terms suggest that the state of nature is always already theatrical.' David Marshall, *The Surprising Effects of Sympathy: Marivaux, Diderot, Rousseau, and Mary Shelley* (Chicago: University of Chicago Press, 1988), 150.

25   https://www.amnesty.org/en/latest/news/2016/05/look-refugees-in-the-eye/, consulted 6 October 2019.

26   See, for example, 'Dove Real Beauty Sketches: You're more beautiful than you think', https://www.youtube.com/watch?v=XpaOjMXyJGk, consulted 6 October 2019.

27   It is worth noting that the horizontality of the '#Look Beyond Borders' *dispositif* is designed to extend beyond the content of the video itself through its viral distribution across social networks.

28   This notion of an economy of the supplement that I allude to here returns us a final time to Rousseau by recalling Derrida's reading of his notion of pity in the *Essay on the Origin of Languages* (1781) as one of the classical avatars for a metaphysics of presence. In *Of Grammatology*, Derrida crystallizes that complex reading in a single, four-word sentence: 'Pity is a voice.' Following that line, what I would wish to say with respect to the logic of '#Look Beyond Borders' is that empathy is a face. Jacques Derrida, *Of Grammatology*, translated by Gayatri Chakravorty Spivak (Baltimore: Johns Hopkins University Press, 1997), 173.

29   Indeed, one of the few sustained readings of the film locates it within the contemporary field of neurosociology, in which 'empathy' has become a central means for suturing the individual to the social. According to Hing Tsang, *Face Value* 'anticipates' an understanding within recent documentary film theory that is 'oriented towards an evolutionary account of intersubjectivity and culture'. Hing Tsang, 'Emotion, Documentary and Van der Keuken's *Face Value*', *Studies in Documentary Film* 5:1 (2011), 17. On this reading, the film offers the spectator a plentitude of occasions for a direct experience of mimetic resonance with the manifold faces it presents, as if

Van der Keuken were conducting his own artistic experiments with 'mirror neurons' at the very cusp of their scientific identification in Parma the year after the film came out. This identification took place in the lab of Giacomo Rizzolatti at the University of Parma and was first reported in Giuseppe di Pellegrino et al., 'Understanding Motor Events: A Neurophysiological Study', *Experimental Brain Research* 91:1 (1992), 176–80.

30   https://www.idfa.nl/en/film/9e526633-8bb2-492f-8d64-8f9c068cdd43/het-masker, consulted 25 August 2019.

31   Fredric Jameson, 'Cognitive Mapping' in *Marxism and the Interpretation of Culture*, edited by Cary Nelson and Lawrence Grossberg (Champaign: University of Illinois Press, 1988).

32   Serge Daney, 'The Cruel Radiance of What Is', translated by Stoffel Debuysere, https://www.diagonalthoughts.com/?p=1450, consulted 12 October 2019. Originally published as 'La Radiation cruelle de ce qui est', *Cahiers du cinéma* 290–1 (July/August 1978), 69–72.

33   Daney, 'The Cruel Radiance of What Is'.

34   Michel Chion, 'Faces and Speech' in *Film, A Sound Art*, translated by Claudia Gorbman (New York: Columbia University Press, 2009), 347–57.

35   Roland Barthes, *The Pleasure of the Text*, translated by Richard Miller (New York: Hill & Wang, 1975), 66–7. For these examples from Chion and Barthes on the interplay between face and voice, I am indebted to Noa Steimatsky's impressive study *The Face on Film* (New York: Oxford University Press, 2017), 68–9.

36   Thomas Elsaesser, 'The Body as Perceptual Surface: The Films of Johan van der Keuken' in *European Cinema: Face to Face with Hollywood* (Amsterdam University Press, 2005), 206.

37   Daney, 'The Cruel Radiance of What Is'.

38   Daney, 'The Cruel Radiance of What Is'.

Sleeping away the Factory, Healing with Time: Gaston Bachelard, the Poetic Imagination and *Testről és lélekről/ On Body and Soul* (2017)

SAIGE WALTON

> The imagination is not (...) the faculty for forming images of reality; it is the faculty for forming images which go beyond reality, which *sing* reality. It is a superhuman faculty.
> Gaston Bachelard[1]

> I think life itself is a mix of realism and dreams. Every day of your life you experience the constant mixture of both.
> Ildikó Enyedi[2]

Outside an unnamed slaughterhouse, a group of cattle stand penned inside a truck. Two anonymous factory workers can be seen and heard talking nearby. The film's focus stays with the cattle, however, moving between their legs and flanks. A cut to the truck's exterior brings with it the close-up of a cow's face. Through sets of blue-grey bars, the cow lifts its head towards the sun, revealing a shining black eye and the fleshy patterns of its muzzle. In the next shot, the brightness of the sun causes a cleaning woman to put aside her mopping. Then, a young blonde woman, Mária (Alexandra Borbély), pauses in a scene of traffic. She looks back towards her reflection in a glass window, ushering in another shift in point of view: now, an older bearded man, Endre (Géza Morcsányi), stands before an office window. Echoing the cow's previous movements, he turns his face towards the sun, closing his eyes to enjoy its warmth. These are the first 'real' world scenes of Ildikó Enyedi's tender *Testről és lélekről/ On Body and Soul* (2017), a film

Paragraph 43.3 (2020): 348–363
DOI: 10.3366/para.2020.0345
© Edinburgh University Press
www.euppublishing.com/para

that approaches human and animal life in parallel, imagining a shared dreamscape between them.

In this article, I draw on Gaston Bachelard's philosophy of time and the poetic imagination to argue that *On Body and Soul* invites us '*to dream well*' in a Bachelardian sense.[3] To date, surprisingly little work has extended Bachelard to the cinema, especially in terms of the connections he puts forth between time, the imagined image and poetic form.[4] In Bachelard's works on time, I posit, we encounter many formative concepts that recur in his writing on the imagination: biodiversity, rhythm, motion, the instant, verticality, novelty, receptivity, repose and 'the creative value of becoming'.[5] Returning to Bachelard's *Intuition of the Instant* and *The Dialectic of Duration*, I draw out some of their continuities with his take on the poetic imagination, using both to underscore the weighting of the instant in *On Body and Soul*.

Inspired by Bachelard's essay 'Poetic Instant and Metaphysical Instant', *Earth and Reveries of Will* and other texts, I then mobilize Bachelard's writings on the crystalline and what he calls 'vertical time' to speak to the doubling of Enyedi's film.[6] For Bachelard, vertical time is poetic, imagined time wherein opposites can coexist and correspondences are formed. In *On Body and Soul*, the film's doubled worlds formally connect and reverse, bringing about repeated encounters with vertical time in the cinema. By attending to crystalline substances (glass, snow, metal), different ways of being and different temporalities (animal, human, poetic), Enyedi forges a poetics of correspondence, encouraging a compassionate gaze on the world and vulnerability in others.

The Difference of the Instant

After establishing a career as a philosopher and a historian of science, Gaston Bachelard became increasingly dissatisfied with the language of scientific rationalism. Equal parts rationalist and romantic, he set about studying the images of poetry and literature as an alternate, even complementary, mode of engagement. Science and poetry should not be conceived as antithetical in Bachelard. During the 1930s he was already invoking poetry and music to advance his non–Bergsonian account of time, also making reference to the 'poetry' of mathematics. During his later period he continued to refer to images of the imagination in quasi–scientific terms, as the basic 'units of reverie'.[7]

As Richard Kearney explains, what Bachelard valued most across the sciences and in poetry was the 'creative ability to break with everyday "facts"'.[8] Whereas new scientific discoveries eventually form established bodies of knowledge, the imagination in Bachelard functions as an inexhaustible font of novelty — a novelty that is activated anew through the poetic image. Here, it is worth remembering the etymological origins of *poiesis* ('to make') and also worth clarifying what the image entails for Bachelard. While invested in developing new literary taxonomies (grouping images in relation to what he regarded as certain common, deep-seated archetypes), it is important to note that Bachelard does not treat the image as a sign. When he refers to the imagination, he is seeking to articulate a more primal mode of contact with the world. Nonetheless, the Bachelardian image is also a created or willed image. As he glosses the poetic image, it 'is always a little above the language of signification (...) poetry puts language in a state of emergence'.[9]

As suggested by this quotation, and across Bachelard's writing in fact, time and the timing of the imagination are fundamental to his poetics.[10] Penned during the 1930s, both *Intuition of the Instant* and *The Dialectic of Duration* mark Bachelard's ardent efforts to counter the reigning philosophy of Henri Bergson. Breaking with the continuity of time and consciousness put forth by Bergson as duration, Bachelard's work advances an inherently discontinuous yet no less vitalistic understanding of time. Contra Bergson, he insists that the present 'does not *pass* (...) we forsake the instant only to find another'.[11] Invoking the measure of time first articulated by his friend Gaston Roupnel, in his 1927 book *Siloë* (an important ecological influence on Bachelard, as I will detail), Bachelard's *Intuition of the Instant* locates 'time's primordial element' in the complexity of the instant, also arguing for 'a diversity of durations and individual times'.[12] In Bachelard's philosophy, the instant (and its later correlate, rhythm) is a plea for temporal, aesthetic and ontological diversity.[13] For Bachelard, via Roupnel, it is the instant that illuminates 'the truly specific character of time' and the present that carries 'the full weight of temporality'.[14]

How might Bachelard's instant be figured in the cinema? Enyedi's *On Body and Soul* offers a rich response to this question, especially given its aesthetic weighting of the instant. The film centres on the healing of two 'damaged' individuals: Endre, the financial director of a Budapest slaughterhouse, and Mária, the factory's new quality-control inspector. Whereas Endre is partially disabled by a crippled hand, Mária is averse to all physical contact. The film implies that the painfully shy as well as mathematically and mnemonically precise Mária exists somewhere on the autism spectrum disorder. According to Enyedi, Endre and Mária are not just introverts. They are wounded. They 'react to an environment (. . .) which is not cut for them — or anybody'.[15] After interviews are conducted with factory employees, the two learn they have been sharing the same dream. In their dreams, they live an alternative existence as animals (as a stag and a doe, respectively).[16] Outside the dreamscape, both can remember this existence, recalling sensations of hunger, foraging, the tasting of a leaf and so on. More than a unique, awkward love story, *On Body and Soul*'s rhythmic, allegorical return to the presence of animals (cattle, deer) and to the dreamed image gestures towards a material spirituality and a temporality that exists outside of everyday human time (a time that can only be imagined).

Bachelard's privileging of the instant (its newness, its presence, its isolation from other instants) carried through to his descriptions of the poetic imagination. One 'must be receptive, receptive to the image at the moment it appears', he writes.[17] In the context of the imagination, the instant resurfaces as what Bachelard calls the 'sudden' image. Attached to a particular creative and temporal dynamic (the instant), the imagined image is framed as a conscious stopgap that interrupts the present: 'it faces the future'.[18]

Even before they are alerted to their shared dreamlife, the first encounter between Endre and Mária is choreographed as a novel, striking moment. Inside the factory, Endre is filmed listening to a colleague complain about repairs. Sounds of laughter drift in from the outside, redirecting his focus. Downstairs, three female workers gather around a large cement pillar. Dressed in industrial whites with individual flashes of colour (a pink hair-tie here, a red shirt there), the young women smoke, talk and laugh with each other. It is not this group who capture Endre's or the film's attention, however. At the far left of the frame Mária stands, perpendicular to the others. Hidden behind the pillar, she tugs at her blouse but does not otherwise step forth. As both sets of conversations continue, ambient ringing sounds begin to echo through the scene. In close-up, Mária is revealed to be standing in a pool of sunlight on the cement. She unclasps her hands, adjusts her hair and steps back, very precisely positioning her feet in line with the shadows cast by the building (Figure 1).

And then, Mária looks up towards Endre, their points of view intersect and the film's sonorous ringing continues. As Bachelard cautions, 'we tend to label "monotonous and regular" only those

Figures 1 and 2. *Testről és lélekről/On Body and Soul* (Ildikó Enyedi, 2017). Courtesy of MUBI.

subtle developments we fail to examine with passionate attention'.[19] Speaking of the wonder that 'can hide behind a placid, grey surface', Enyedi suggests that she, too, seeks to instil an attitude of attentiveness in the viewer.[20] Through its combination of architecture, framing, sunlight, gesture, music and sound, this scene can be affiliated with the novelty of the instant, so valued by Bachelard. Lyrically redirecting the focus of Endre, Mária as well as the viewer, Enyedi punctures the anticipated rhythms and routine of the factory.

From the beginning, Endre and Mária are singled out as being separate to others but audiovisually connected to each other. Oftentimes, intense ringing sounds accompany the pair when they are brought into each other's orbit. These pellucid sounds pervade the depiction of animal life in the dreamscape, suggesting porosity between the two worlds. Yet Enyedi's foregrounding of novelty is by no means limited to dreams. Tiny, affectively charged instants and heightened poetic moments recur across *On Body and Soul*. As Mária reaches for a glass in the cafeteria, her hand visibly halts in mid-air, preternaturally aware of the fall of Endre's footsteps behind her. The film pauses *with* Mária here, temporarily frozen in place. Shifting to a profile shot of Mária (seen from the rear), Enyedi foregrounds her sudden instant of awareness. In close-up, we are privy to Mária's slight movements and her flickering glance. By treating the seemingly unremarkable as a source of the poetic (both within and outside of the dreamscape), Enyedi's film embraces the temporality of the instant and its potential. Through cinematically striking images and sounds, lyricism, surprise and vitality are all figured as a moment of temporal rupture, a 'radical novelty of instants'.[21]

In *Intuition of the Instant*, Bachelard maintains that the instant is not just about the (discontinuous) nature of time. The instant is an instance of will — ushering in a moment of considered, implicitly ethical attention. In these terms, the instant signals an intensification of consciousness. Here again, Bachelard's polemic against Bergson is manifest. Whereas Bergsonian evolution is attached to life's 'natural' motor (the *élan vital*), Bachelard's instant is attached to human beings 'judging, choosing and acting'.[22] For Bachelard, the instant imparts a philosophy of the act, meaning that 'we must return to clear acts of consciousness in order to detect the instant'.[23] From the moment of his first seeing Mária, standing apart from the others, Endre is galvanized to approach her. Following the pair's first awkward encounter, Mária seeks out Endre but hesitates before the cafeteria's glass door. The workers inside are presented as indistinct shapes and out-of-focus colours, moving across the glass. Enyedi nonetheless shows Mária's face in crystal-clear relief. We see her moment of uncertainty, set against the opening and closing door. As Jean-François Perraudin describes it, Bachelard's instant 'involves the tightening of consciousness which, in a state of sudden tension, will generate an act', even an existential rupture.[24] As a musical ringing rises, Mária decides to enter. In the next shot, the camera shifts to occupy her previous position, its vision holding on the swinging door. An oneiric, shimmering sound begins — as if Mária had just crossed a magical threshold through a small-scale act of bravery.

Individually, Endre and Mária are often presented through glassed, enframed, windowed or barred views, visually recalling the film's opening shots of penned cattle. By contrast, their encounters inside the factory are imaged and imagined as a 'rupture of being': an existential rupture that is figured sonically, gesturally and spatially.[25] In this regard,

On Body and Soul accords with Bachelard's own insistence on the instant as a sudden 'flare-up' of the imagination.[26] For Bachelard, the imagined image hinges upon novelty, creativity and newness. As a moment of willed attention, also, it harbours the potential to spark endless new beginnings: other ways of being.

For Enyedi, suggesting the 'interference between body and soul' was essential to the composition of *On Body and Soul*.[27] In these terms, it was crucial to focus on 'things that were just about the body' while simultaneously 'putting the accent on the soul'.[28] Time and again, Enyedi's novel shot compositions ask us to attend to a moment of embodied vulnerability on screen: from the touching shot of a cow's face (its black-tagged ear marking out its fate) to Mária, stepping back into the shadows or hesitating before a door. When we tighten our focus on the instant, as Bachelard writes, it 'will suddenly illuminate the mind'.[29] Like the sunlight that shines, intermittently, on the dull cement slaughterhouse, Mária, Endre and the film's animals are all portrayed as vulnerable 'souls', linked to the images, sounds and textures of nature.

Crystalline Reveries and Vertical Time

After making the transition from science to poetics, Bachelard sought 'a deeper *poiesis* wherein imagination and reality make and remake each other'.[30] Of particular relevance to the cinema, I believe, is the fact that there is no one fixed image or mode of the imagination for Bachelard. Some imagined images are dynamic and ephemeral (the 'spectacle of fire or water or sky'); others are more primal (weighted images of earth and mud).[31] Some images are cosmic in scope while others inhere in a childhood cupboard. Reveries interrupt clock time, bringing about relaxed sensations of drifting and calm. Still further potential for diversity exists through the propensity of the imagination to form imaginary compounds (the admixture of water and earth, say). In addition, Bachelard identifies two different axes to the imagination: the formal and the material. Whereas the formal imagination is concerned with surface appearances and representational concepts (form as it is commonly understood and relatable), the material imagination is steeped in 'the richness and density of matter'.[32]

Despite Bachelard's basis in literary poetics and his praising of the material over the formal, I think we can identify a number of *formal* constants to his writing that are equally transposable to film. Alongside his cataloguing of the natural elements (fire, water, air, two volumes on earth), the other crucial 'element' at work in Bachelard is the poeticizing impulse. In *Earth and Reveries of Will*, the will-to-poetry is symbolized through the figure of the artist-craftsman, working to free the precious gemstone from the rock. For Bachelard, the imagined image 'may *precede* perception, initiating an adventure in perception'.[33] Like cinema itself, then, the Bachelardian imagination is in touch with the material make-up of the world even as it creatively de-forms and re-forms it. Instead of 'adjusting to the reality that is given', it aspires 'toward new images'.[34] It expresses and renews existence through poetic form.

Also complementing Enyedi's *On Body and Soul* is Bachelard's dialectical sensibility, often articulated as a poetic doubling, ambivalence or tension. In *Water and Dreams*, the philosopher goes so far as to assert that the doubling of matter is a 'primordial law of the imagination'.[35] As early as *Intuition of the Instant*, though, Bachelard was already mobilizing the instant to articulate 'a felt synthesis of contraries'.[36] As I mentioned previously, Roupnel's ideas exerted an implicit ecological influence on Bachelard's time-based philosophy. Via Roupnel, Bachelard speaks of the countryside, landscapes and vineyards, invoking 'the hour' known by strawberries, peaches and grapes.[37] Through Roupnel, he was prompted to discern different levels of duration and different rhythms of existence (human and nonhuman). In Bachelard's writings on the imagination of earth, he invokes Roupnel through his identification of different (nonhuman) time scales. Writing of the struggle between 'breakdown and effervescence (. . .) between dust and bubbles', Bachelard posits that different material temporalities work 'matter dialectically', just 'like systole and diastole work the heart'.[38]

In extending Bachelard to the cinema, I find it noteworthy that Bachelard tends to associate the more fundamental imagery of the imagination with a sensing of time.[39] In *Earth and Reveries of Will*, he speaks, beautifully, of reveries that are borne of crystalline matter: the imagination of gemstones, diamonds, salty minerals, rocky caves and crystallized forests. Whereas the crystal-image in Gilles Deleuze's philosophy has been used to capture a complex temporal layering in film (an image in which the actual and the virtual, human and nonhuman temporalities coexist), Bachelard's crystal is imbued with a different temporal and aesthetic sentiment.[40] By way of the crystal, Bachelard's instant as an instant of attentiveness shines forth once more. Instead of temporal stratification (the crystalline layering of time), Bachelard's crystal emblematizes suspended, poetic time. What entrancing, strange 'reveries occur through crystals', he writes, 'with crystalline matter at once a single instant frozen in time and an eternity!'[41] Through the crystalline, as Kearney details, 'Bachelard holds that we create and we disclose *at one and the same time*'.[42] As a created or willed image, the crystalline discloses the atemporality of imagined time alongside a 'materialism of purity'.[43]

To imagine the purity of the 'soul', *On Body and Soul* returns to and repeats the elemental images, textures and sounds of a snowy dreamscape. Following the film's opening black screen, crystalline sounds echo and shudder, sonically reminiscent of the ringing of a glass. Birdsong is introduced and darkness gives way to a serene, glacial forest, dense with silvery-grey trees and falling snow. In the distance, two deer (Endre and Mária's allegorical doubles) make their way through the woods. The musical score ceases and a nature-based chorus follows, composed of intermittent birdcalls, the treading of the deer's hooves and snowfall, heard partially melting as it makes contact with the earth. It 'is not by chance that the dream sequences are realistic', director Enyedi states. She wanted to foreground 'a real wood, with real winter sounds', at once luminous and concrete. Likewise, the animals contained therein are 'very much real, they are not the deer of fairytales. They do everyday things.'[44]

As the two animals become aware of each other's presence, the buck begins to sniff at and nudge the doe. In turn, the film's vision shifts closer to reveal the two deer's differently coloured markings (rust, brown, fawn, touches of white) and the tiny flecks of snow that coat their pelts. The buck rests its antlered head on the doe's back but she refuses his advances, exiting off screen before he slowly ambles after her. Suddenly, a series of incongruous metal sounds erupt: thud, thud, thud. The life of the factory filters through the image. A shot of muddied animal hooves follows. The free-roaming deer are transmuted into their 'real' world counterpart: dirtied cattle, penned and waiting to be processed into meat at the factory.

In interviews, Enyedi openly acknowledges the influence of poetry upon her film's doubled imagery, citing the work of the Hungarian poet Ágnes Nemes Nagy as a particular source of inspiration.[45] In this regard, *On Body and Soul*'s prologue and its other scenes featuring the deer were intended as a non-verbal, poetic provocation to the viewer. By moving from the natural 'grace' of the deer in the forest to the implied weight and heaviness of bovines in the factory, Enyedi sought to align Endre and Mária's love, rest and healing with natural, even suggestively metaphysical, forces.[46] Repeated, unflinching shots of weighted, penned or suspended cattle were intended to invert the film's gentle rendering of the deer, encouraging a compassionate gaze. Following the film's opening introduction to the penned cattle, a long take follows in which a cow is clamped with metal chains then hoisted into the air. Abruptly, Enyedi cuts to the imagery of suspended beef carcasses, smoothly and efficiently gliding by on a metallic conveyor belt. Crucially, the clinical, mechanized labour that we see inside the factory is not that of 'some archaic, blood-soaked abattoir'. Instead, the factory is presented as a 'neat, well organized, modern workplace'. As Enyedi comments: 'It is the mirror of our Western society.'[47]

On the factory's lower floors, mechanical bells signal the arrival of new cattle for processing. Upstairs, clock faces adorn the walls, phones ring, heels click and people bustle back and forth. The filming of labour (including scenes of animal butchery) alternates with the workers taking regular coffee breaks. Time is scheduled. A bull 'mating is done in three minutes', Endre tells a visitor. Unlike the linear time of the factory, the dreamscape occupies an indeterminate temporality. We do not know where the oneiric vista is located nor can we anticipate when it will resurface. 'Every true poem can reveal the elements of suspended time, meterless time', Bachelard maintains of the poetic.[48]

In his essay 'Poetic Instant and Metaphysical Instant' (a neglected prelude to his dedicated works on the imagination), Bachelard brings the instant together with the time of poetry. Here again, he invokes a temporal pluralism. For example, he speaks of social time (the organized time of people), phenomenal time (the time of things) and vital time (the time of life, such as the beating of one's heart). These temporalities all coexist within horizontal time: 'everyday time, which sweeps along horizontally with the streaming waters and the blowing winds'.[49] Poetry runs counter to all these durations. According to Bachelard, it constitutes vertical time (created or imagined time), refusing the sequential. As it need not adhere to 'real'-world dynamics, also, the vertical time of poetry has the potential to lift 'the individual out of the ordinary flow of time'.[50] Through its non-linear, charged images, poetry enacts a momentary metaphysics: 'the vision of a universe and the secret of a soul — an insight into being and objects'.[51]

As the slaughterhouse shuts down for the evening, its machinery whirs into silence. We see Mária switching off her own solitary lamp, followed by other workers exiting. In the next moment, Enyedi shifts focus to attend to the factory's cattle, standing quietly in the dark. A cow raises its head, unaware of the beginning or end of the working day. The camera holds on the cattle, gently breathing and moving in the darkness. In the next shot, we see Endre working into the night. Sounds of water seep through the scene, sonically anticipating the close-up of deer hooves on snow that follows. Once more, the industrial lives of Endre, Mária and the cattle reverse into the restful environs and alternate temporality of the deer (Figure 2). In another sequence, the deer are filmed drinking from a stream in the forest. Here, the film takes the time to show us the detail of the deer's existence: the opaque grains of ice that cling to their hooves; the greenery caught in the buck's antlers, the doe's white, vaporous breath. After the deer vacate the frame, a set of heavy metal doors can be heard sliding open. Another shift at the slaughterhouse has commenced.

For Bachelard, vertical time is to be celebrated for its ability to escape linearity, generate ambivalence and conjoin opposites (for instance, likening the light of diamonds with the light of stars). Imagining a correspondence between phenomena is crucial. Whereas clock time shapes, disciplines, divides and regulates, vertical time bridges difference, 'invoking deeper metaphysical connections that cannot be experienced in chronological time'.[52] Not surprisingly, Bachelard's writing singles out Baudelaire (the famous French poet of correspondences) for his 'summary of sentient being in a single moment'.[53] Like Baudelaire, Bachelard sees the poet/writer (and, I would add, the filmmaker) as being able to bring forth 'a true material correspondence' between things, a correspondence that is hastened by the mobile, synthesizing powers of the imagination.[54]

Writing of crystalline matter, Bachelard posits that the crystal offers nothing less than a 'snapshot of the universe' — an instant and an eternity, it teaches us to listen to 'the tranquil pauses of poetry'.[55] As indicated by its prologue, together with its many other lyrically charged instants, *On Body and Soul* is suffused with tranquil pauses. Such moments work to generate 'a harmonic relationship between two opposites': the forest and the factory, the human and the animal, the time of love, poetry and dreaming versus the time of labour.[56] In *On Body and Soul*, crystalline matter abounds: the recurrence of ice, snow, glass and metal. According to Enyedi, the film's 'waken hours' were deliberately stylized as abstract to help convey the 'building of a mythical relationship'.[57] Throughout, geometrically precise, glassed and translucent compositions alternate with the pristine forest. Both dream and waking life are shot through with atmospheric ringing and shimmering sounds. Just as the instant erupts inside the factory (instigating novelty, lyricism and surprise), so do the elemental forces of nature filter through the film's industrial spaces (as pale sunlight or sudden winds). In adopting Bachelard's thinking for the cinema, however, we cannot afford to delimit vertical time to representational dreamscapes nor even to this film's collection of dreamt, restful moments. As Bachelard insists, the 'vertical dimension that presides over the poetic' accumulates well-ordered simultaneities, giving rise to its own 'internal order'.[58] All of *On Body and Soul* partakes of vertical time and is imbued with its own crystalline order, achieved through the imaging of poetic correspondence.

In Bachelard, crystalline reveries illustrate 'the beauties of the instant, the many beautiful brief changes that are possible'.[59] The later are only possible, he insists, if the 'dreamer dreams *attentively*'.[60] To harness the deep-seated powers of the imagination for the cinema — what I am suggesting here as an encounter with vertical time — the crystalline must be fashioned with great care. Akin to a 'reverie before (. . .) a single diamond', such well-crafted, willed images encourage a similar attitude of care, curiosity and attentiveness in the viewer.[61] For Enyedi, staging the interference between 'body' and 'soul' meant crafting images of fragility and vulnerability, a trait that is shared by animals and humans alike.

Conclusion: Dreaming Well and the Cinema

This article has considered how Bachelard's writing on the imagination continued to be shaped by his thinking on time, especially his notion of the instant. In bringing Bachelard's time-based philosophy and his poetic philosophy together with the cinema, it is possible to see how the relationship between film and imagination might be extended beyond analyses of character-based reveries, the depiction of dreams or the internal imaginings of the viewer. Through its alternating formal dynamics, its shifting focus between species, its foregrounding of the instant and its crystalline lyricism, *On Body and Soul* heeds Bachelard's advice to 'dream well'.[62] Only by 'sojourning long enough with novel images', he reminds us, can we hope to experience the kind of imagined images that renew our 'real' existence.[63] For Enyedi, too, the material world needs to be supplemented with the poetic.

At the end of *On Body and Soul*, Endre and Mária sit together as a couple over breakfast, adjusting to each other's daily habits. They realize that they cannot remember their dream from the previous night or if they dreamed at all. In the shot that directly follows, the forest appears, thick with snow and *sans* animal life. In the quiet, two drops of water fall into a large pool before the frame erupts with a pure, almost blinding, white light. Somewhere in the forest, in a moment of vertical time, the deer are now dreaming.

NOTES

1 Gaston Bachelard, *Water and Dreams: An Essay on the Imagination of Matter*, translated by Edith R. Farrell (Dallas: Dallas Institute Publications, 1983 [1942]), 16, emphasis in original.

2 Ildikó Enyedi, 'Comments from Writer-Director Ildikó Enyedi', *On Body and Soul* Press Kit, https://releases.mubi.com/onbodyandsoul/wp-content/uploads/sites/5/2017/11/OBAS-PressKit-digital.pdf, consulted 7 October 2019.

3 Gaston Bachelard, *Earth and Reveries of Will: An Essay on the Imagination of Matter*, translated by Kenneth Haltman (Dallas: Dallas Institute Publications, 2002 [1943]), 2, emphasis in original. For Bachelard, the dialectical activities of the intellect and the imagination help to cultivate well-being. Bachelard's main works on time include *Intuition of the Instant*, translated by Eileen Rizo-Patron (Evanston: Northwestern University Press, 2013 [1932]) and *The Dialectic of Duration*, translated by Mary McAllester Jones (Manchester: Clinamen Press, 2000 [1936]). Dated 1938–60, Bachelard's writings on the imagination run from the publication of *The Psychoanalysis of Fire* through to *The Poetics of Reverie*. The selected works that I focus on include Bachelard's *Water* and Gaston Bachelard, *The Poetics of Space*, translated by Maria Jolas (Boston: Beacon Press, 1994 [1958]). For a useful overview of Bachelard's studies of the imagination, see Edward K. Kaplan, 'Gaston Bachelard's Philosophy of the Imagination: An Introduction', *Philosophy and Phenomenological Research* 33:1 (1972), 1–24.

4 Bachelard's lyrically seductive prose is often quoted, yet few film and media scholars engage with his writings in a sustained way. On reverie in animation, see Scott Bukatman, *The Poetics of Slumberland: Animated Spirits and Animating Spirit* (Berkeley: University of California Press, 2012). On Bachelard's 'intimate immensity', see Amelie Hastie, 'Cinema of Compassion', *LOLA* 4 (2013), http://www.lolajournal.com/4/compassion.html, consulted 1 October 2019. More recently, my own work has examined the connections between Bachelard's work on the elements, mood and the materiality of horror. See Saige Walton, 'Air, Atmosphere, Environment: Film Mood, Folk Horror and *The VVitch*', *Screening the Past* 43 (2018), http://www.screeningthepast.com/2018/02/air-atmosphere-environment-film-mood-folk-horror-and-the-vvitch/, consulted 1 October

2019. On Bachelard's relevance to ecological cinema, see also Ludo de Roo, 'Elemental Imagination and Film Experience', *Projections* 13:2 (2019), 58–79.

5   Bachelard, *Dialectic*, 24.

6   Gaston Bachelard, 'Poetic Instant and Metaphysical Instant' in *Intuition*, 58–63. This essay is translated as 'The Poetic Moment and the Metaphysical Moment' in the posthumously published *The Right to Dream* (Dallas: Dallas Institute Publications, 1988 [1971]), 173–8. I opt for the former title to foreground its continuities with the instant.

7   Gaston Bachelard, *The Poetics of Reverie: Childhood, Language and the Cosmos*, translated by Daniel Russell (Boston: Beacon Press, 1971 [1960]), 176.

8   Richard Kearney, *Poetics of Imagining: Modern to Post-Modern* (Edinburgh: Edinburgh University Press, 1998), 97.

9   Bachelard, *Poetics of Space*, xxvii.

10 Bachelard's philosophy also emphasizes the time the image takes to take root within and be worked over by the mind. This temporality is associated with botanical and terrestrial imagery. See *Water*, 3 and *Earth*, 224.

11 Bachelard, *Intuition*, 28, emphasis in original. Here, it is not my intention to dispute Bergsonism but to establish Bachelard's interrelated thinking on time. See Perraudin for a fascinating discussion of Bachelard's relationship with Bergson. Jean François Perraudin, 'Bachelard's "Non-Bergsonianism"', translated by Eileen Rizo-Patron in *Adventures in Phenomenology: Gaston Bachelard*, edited by Eileen Rizo-Patron, Edward S. Casey and James M. Wirth (Albany: State University of New York, 2017), 29–48.

12 Bachelard, *Intuition*, 8. Roupnel was Bachelard's colleague at the University of Dijon (1930–40). In his spiritually inflected *Siloë*, Roupnel postulates 'a "Universal Spirit" as immanent, transcendental, perpetually recurring (. . .) apprehended in a fleeting instant or moment' that is rooted within nature. Philip Whalen, 'Gaston Roupnel' in *French Historians, 1900–2000*, edited by Philip Daileader and Philip Whalen (Oxford: Wiley-Blackwell Press, 2010), 534. *Siloë*'s title derives its name from the Gospel story of Siloam in which a blind man's sight is restored. On the therapeutic connections between Roupnel and Bachelard, see Perraudin, 'Bachelard's "Non-Bergsonianism"' and Mary McAllester Jones, 'The Redemptive Instant: Bachelard on the Epistemological and Existential Value of Surprise', *Philosophy Today* 47: Issue Supplement (2003), 124–31.

13 Bachelard equates rhythm with 'a system of instants'. *Dialectic*, 21.

14 Bachelard, *Intuition*, 12.

15 Enyedi, 'Comments'.

16 There are suggestions that other factory workers have animal counterparts. One dreams of himself as a blue horse, for example.

17 Bachelard, *Poetics of Space*, xv.

18 Bachelard, *Poetics of Space*, xxxiv.

19   Bachelard, *Intuition*, 7.

20   Benjamin B, '*On Body and Soul*: Interview with Director Ildikó Enyedi', *American Cinematographer* Blog, https://ascmag.com/blog/the-film-book/on-body-and-soul-director-ildiko-enyedi, consulted 1 October 2019.

21   Bachelard, *Intuition*, 37.

22   Bachelard, *Dialectic*, 10. An interesting parallel with Eugène Minkowski can be invoked here as he advances a Bergsonian-influenced 'personal élan', lost in certain mental disorders. On Minkowski's influence on Bachelard, see *Poetics of Space* and *Poetics of Reverie*.

23   Bachelard, *Intuition*, 11–12.

24   Perraudin, 'Bachelard's "Non-Bergsonianism"', 35.

25   Bachelard, *Intuition*, 7.

26   Bachelard, *Poetics of Space*, xviii.

27   Benjamin, '*On Body and Soul*'.

28   Benjamin, '*On Body and Soul*'.

29   Bachelard, *Intuition*, 12.

30   Kearney, *Poetics of Imagining*, 97.

31   Bachelard, *Earth*, 2.

32   Bachelard, *Water*, 10.

33   Bachelard, *Earth*, 3. Bachelard's phrasing calls to mind the experimental filmmaker Stan Brakhage.

34   Kaplan, 'Gaston Bachelard's Philosophy', 4.

35   Bachelard, *Water*, 11.

36   Bachelard, *Intuition*, 56.

37   Kristupas Sabolius, 'Rhythm and Reverie: On the Temporality of the Imagination in Bachelard' in *Adventures in Phenomenology: Gaston Bachelard*, edited by Eileen Rizo-Patron, Edward S. Casey and James M. Wirth (Albany: State University of New York, 2017), 66.

38   Bachelard, *Earth*, 67.

39   Unlike the formal imagination, the material imagination is granted 'time to work upon (...) matter'. Bachelard, *Water*, 11.

40   For a nuanced discussion of Deleuze, the nonhuman and the crystalline, see Laura McMahon, 'Beyond the Human Body: Claire Denis' Ecologies', *Alphaville: Journal of Film and Screen Media* 7 (2014), http://www.alphavillejournal.com/Issue7/HTML/ArticleMcMahon.html, consulted 10 October 2019.

41   Bachelard, *Earth*, 232.

42   Richard Kearney, 'Bachelard and the Epiphanic Instant', *Philosophy Today* 52: Supplement (2008), 41.

43   Bachelard, *Earth*, 226.

44   Enyedi, 'Comments'.

45 Nemes Nagy's poetry relies heavily on the imagery of nature (ice, trees) to convey myth and also spirituality through worldly objects and things.

46 Benjamin, '*On Body and Soul*'. The philosophy of Simone Weil also exerted a strong influence on Enyedi's film.

47 Enyedi, 'Comments'.

48 Bachelard, *Intuition*, 58.

49 Bachelard, *Intuition*, 58.

50 Bachelard, *Right to Dream*, 177. Verticality is a constant motif in Bachelard.

51 Bachelard, *Intuition*, 58.

52 Kearney, 'Bachelard', 39.

53 Bachelard, *Right to Dream*, 177.

54 Bachelard, *Earth*, 225.

55 Bachelard, *Earth*, 239.

56 Bachelard, *Intuition*, 59.

57 Enyedi, 'Comments'.

58 Bachelard, *Intuition*, 59. The crystalline also bespeaks a formal unity of design. See Bachelard, *Earth*, 227.

59 Bachelard, *Earth*, 228.

60 Bachelard, *Earth*, 226.

61 Bachelard, *Earth*, 228.

62 Bachelard, *Earth*, 2.

63 Bachelard, *Earth*, 4.

Cinematic Imaging and Imagining through the Lens of Buddhism

Victor Fan

All phenomena are like
A dream, an illusion, a bubble and a shadow.
Like a dew drop and a flash of lightning,
Thus should you view them.[1]
Vajracchedikā Prajñāpāramitā Sūtra, §32

In Buddhist philosophy, imaging and imagining are neither the same nor different, neither *not* the same nor *not* different. On a day-to-day basis, we, as human beings, often consider imaging as an operation of the consciousness, a process in which vision — our neurological system's bare cognition of a field of photons — is turned into recognition. Thus, the resulting image *out there* confirms our knowledge of reality, sense-certainty and subjectivity. The image, and the sentient body that *images*, are also believed to have their own existential values. Meanwhile, imagining is considered a mental process that relies on memories of previous perceptions and recognitions, *seemingly* without the aid of any external sensorial stimulations. The resulting imagination, or even the imagining mind, appears to be ungraspable, transient and non-existent. However, what makes us so certain that those sense data that we claim as being external to our body, which constitute the difference between imaging and imagining, are not part of our imagination?

The oft-undiscernible boundary between imaging and imagining is especially apparent in our cinematic experience. The cinematographic image is initiated out of an interaction between a field of photons emanated from a screen and a neurological system that processes them as sense data. Yet, the resulting bare cognition, once being recognized as an image, is not taken *im-mediately* (without mediation) as a field

Paragraph 43.3 (2020): 364–380
DOI: 10.3366/para.2020.0346
© Edinburgh University Press
www.euppublishing.com/para

of vision; rather, it is recognized as a plane of existence on which we dwell, with other sentient beings and objects with which we constitute an *agencement* (layout) of interdependent relationships. In the cinema, we therefore at once image and imagine. It is in this light that Christian Metz calls the cinematographic image an imaginary signifier: a sign (in the Symbolic order) that enables the sentient body, in its 'sub-motor and super-perceptive state', to configure a disorganized and incoherent field of sensory stimulants (the Real) into an Imaginary order, with a set of codes that is in-formed by the symbolic arrangement of the cinematic apparatus itself.[2]

According to Buddhist philosophy, imaging and imagining are both regarded as a process called *saṅkhāra/saṃskara* (formation). When the six *viññāṇas/vijñānas* (consciousnesses) — of the eyes, ears, nose, tongue, body and mind — are in operation, the cognitive process of identifying and differentiating (*nāma*) one form from another enables the origination and existence of *saḷāyatanas/ṣaḍāyatanas* (sense bases or sensory-perceptual organs, i.e. internal forms).[3] Meanwhile, this cognitive process also posits those forms in the sensory-perceptual field as external forms (*rūpas*). In this article, I argue that imaging in Buddhism refers not only to the formational process of an image *out there*, but also these external forms' interdependent relationship with the internal forms. Likewise, imagining refers not only to the formational process of an image *in here*, but also to how these imaginations actively constitute the body's relationship with the larger milieu *out there*.[4] In the second half of this article, I analyse how the interdependent relationship between imaging and imagining is configured textually and in the overall cinematic experience in Bi Gan's *Diqiu zuihou de yewan/Long Day's Journey into Night* (2018).

Dependent Originations

The belief that imaging and imagining are two different operations is founded upon a perceptual difference between self and other, interiority and exteriority. Buddhist philosophy puts into question this fundamental divide by proposing an idea called dependent originations.

The *Saṃyuktāgama* [Connected discourses, SA-298], the earliest collection of the oral traditions circulated before the Third Buddhist Council (*c.* 250 BCE), defines dependent originations as: 'The existence of a consequent depends on the existence of a cause-condition; the origination of the consequent depends on the origination of that cause-condition.'[5] The subjects and objects of this statement are neither the consequent nor the cause-condition – that is, a living being, inanimate object, affective state, action or event. Rather, they refer to a perception and conception of a state of being (existence) and a process of becoming (origination). Hence, a more accurate way to understand this statement is: 'The perception and conception of a state of being depend on the perception and conception of another state of being; the perception and conception of a process of becoming depend on the perception and conception of another process of becoming.'

In Sanskrit, the term *hetu-pratyata* (cause-condition) refers to the interdependency between a direct cause and a layout of conditions. It means that, perceptually and conceptually, the existence and origination of a direct cause must depend on the existences and originations of other conditions.[6] For example, the existence and origination of light particles are fundamental to the existence and origination of a cinematographic image. Yet, the existence and origination of the image depend on the existence and origination of a layout of technical, physio-psychic, historical and socio-political conditions. Each of these conditions is dependent on another layout of conditions. Perceptually and conceptually, one condition is dependent on another layout of conditions ad infinitum, thus it is impossible to perceive and conceptualize the existence of an unmoved mover unless we violate the axiom of dependent originations.[7]

As an example, let us look at the core components of the anthropotechnical assemblage on which the existence and origination of a cinematographic image depends. For my analysis, I choose an arbitrary starting point: *objective reality*. From a technical perspective, it can be defined as an electromagnetic field in-formed by a layout of photons and other waves and particles, whose momentum is polarized into a sinusoidal plane that is represented perceptually and conceptually as a spatiotemporal cone.[8] The existence and origination of this analytical starting point, which seem to be posited in objective reality, depend on the existence and origination of perception and conception. In other words, what we take for granted as an *objective reality* — an electromagnetic field — is already a perceptual-conceptual configuration: an image/imagination. In Buddhism, this is called *ālambana-pratyata* (foundational condition).[9]

In an anthropotechnical layout we call the cinematic apparatus, this objective reality is captured by the camera optically, stored either analogically or digitally, and reassembled as a spatiotemporal cone that is then transmitted through our optico-neurological organs in order to form a vision. The existence and origination of each condition in this layout depend on the existence and origination of a contiguous one. In Buddhism, this relationship is called *anantara-pratyata* (seed condition) and *samanatara-pratyata* (matching condition). These two conditions are often combinedly called a condition of contiguity.[10] These conditions explain the formational process of bare cognition, but not how this visual field and the body are recognized as an image-consciousness.

For Buddhist scholars, this process of turning from bare cognition to recognition is called *saṅkhāra/saṃskara* (formation). Formation is an operation of the *viññāṇa/vijñāna* (consciousness), which is called *nāmarūpa* (naming and in-forming). *Nāma* refers to the cognitive process of identifying and differentiating one form from another. The existence and origination of this process depend on the existence and origination of *saḷāyatanas/ṣaḍāyatanas* (sense bases or sensory-perceptual organs, i.e. internal forms). *Rūpa* refers to the process of positing those forms in the sensory-perceptual field as external forms, which maintain a distance from the internal forms.[11]

For Buddhist philosophers, consciousness at this stage is not a singular and unified operation. Rather, each sensory-perceptual process is a discrete consciousness. Thus, there are consciousnesses of the eyes, ears, nose, tongue, body and mind (here, the mind refers to the thought-process). Neurosciences have by now located these acts of naming and in-forming at the lateral geniculate nucleus (LGN) and the primary visual cortexes (V1–6). However, they have not yet been able to explicate where these abilities or impetuses come from and how a bare cognition is recognized as an objective reality vis-à-vis the body.

Scholars Kañukurunde Ñaṇananda and Yin Shun identify respectively that the generation of *vedanās* (sensations and affections) is the turning point between bare cognition and recognition.[12] The existence and origination of sensations and affections depend on the existence and origination of the perceptual-conceptual difference between internal and external forms. Such a difference provides the condition for the *phassa/sparśa* (contact) between internal forms and their external counterparts, thus producing sensations and affections. This is what Ñaṇananda calls the subjective phase of the sensory-perceptual process. Affections can be pleasurable, unpleasurable or indifferent, which produces a *taṇhā/tṛṣṇā* (longing) for the perpetuity of these feelings. Such longing produces an *upādāna* (attachment) to the *bhava* (existence) of all forms. Thus, forms, which were subjectivized in the phase of *vedanās,* are now projected outward as the *objective subjective.*[13]

Existence of a form is conditioned upon the existence of a layout of other forms that serve as its *adhipati-pratyata* (dominant condition). It means that the existence of a form only lasts as long as the dominant condition exists. Moreover, Buddhist scholars argue that forms are originated and extinguished from one *kṣaṇa* (smallest unit of time) to another. A form that seems to persist in time is in fact a sequence of contiguously reproduced forms that we misrecognize as one. Thus, forms are by default *anicca/anitya* (impermanent), which goes through cycles of *jāti* (birth or origination) and *jarāmaraṇa* (decay, and death or extinction).[14]

The cinematographic image, in this sense, is never recognized immediately as a layout of existent beings and objects. Let us say that we are in a darkened cinema watching a film, where our sensory-perceptual organs are drawn predominantly to the visual field on the screen and the audio field that envelops us. In such an environment, the LGN and V1–6 will configure an attentive gaze by limiting the muscular movements of our eyes and body, thus enabling the optical elements on screen and the forms they represent as the dominant condition on which our sensations, affections, longing, attachment, and sense of existence depend. However, even in this situation, a triple recognition is in operation, which involves: (1) the recognition of the optical image as a physical form that exists and maintains a distance from the perceiving body; (2) the reliance of the forms on screen as the dominant condition on which (the existence and origination of) the internal forms depend generates an identification between the sensory-perceptual body and the technical body (especially the camera); these two bodies, however, were in fact one during the bare cognition stage; and (3) the recognition of the audio-visual field as an existent objective reality, which produces an identification between the body and the body of the protagonist, whose point of view the camera often assumes in the image. The second and third recognitions are what Metz calls primary and secondary identifications.[15]

At this point, I want to bring our attention to the relationship between the starting point and endpoint of this formational process. The endpoint of this process is the existence and origination of an image-consciousness, whereas the starting point — what we often taken for granted as *objective reality* — is also a perceptual-conceptual formation — that is, an image-consciousness. The difference is that, in the beginning, the existences and originations of smell, taste and touch depend on the direct contact between the external and internal forms. By the end, these three sensations and affections are, as Vivian Sobchack argues, supplemented synaesthetically by the operation of the consciousnesses.[16] In other words, the entire process of becoming is known in Buddhism as *papañca* (perceptual-conceptual proliferation), which is *anatta/anātman* (*śūnya*, or empty of existential value). Our unawareness of this is called *avijjā/avidyā* (ignorance — or ignorance of ignorance), which is the impetus for the cyclical operation of this process, often called the twelve *nidānas* (interdependent relationships). In other words, this entire process of imaging is merely a conceptual-perceptual operation — that is, imaging *is* imagining.

Modulation and Mediation

But then, if imaging and imagining are perceptual-conceptual proliferations, where lies the impetus that motivates these proliferations and determines the codes in which these proliferations operate?

This question was first debated by Buddhist scholars on the relationship between a seed condition and a matching condition. Perceptually and conceptually, the origination, existence and extinction of a condition takes place in one *kṣaṇa*. When we say that the origination and existence of a matching condition depends on the origination and existence of a seed condition, we give the impression that when the seed condition is extinguished, a code remains, which actively rewrites the matching condition as a reproduction, assimilation or retribution of and to the seed. If the originations and existences of the seed and matching conditions are immediately contiguous, we will get the impression of temporal continuity. Yet, if the originations and existences of these two conditions appear to be spatiotemporally discrete, we will get the impression that the consequence of the seed is deferred, delayed and displaced, a phenomenon known as *kamma/karma*.[17]

As a perceptual-conceptual phenomenon, *karma* seems to suggest that dependent originations are mediated by *bījas* (seeds) that function as potentialities. For scholars from the Sarvāstivāda (School of the existence of everything), potentialities are impulses that remain dormant and formless after the extinction of the seed conditions themselves, until they are activated by other conditions and actualized as a matching condition. Potentialities regulate the form of the matching condition by defining the codes in which the consequence is written. These codes, however, can be reconfigured by the originations and existences of other conditions that render the origination and existence of the matching condition. Sarvāstivāda scholars emphasize that these potentialities are *avyākata/avyākṛta* (unmarked by neither good nor evil). Hence, whether the matching condition is good or evil, benevolent or malevolent, depends on the dominant conditions at the time of its actualization.[18]

Even though potentialities are dormant, formless and unmarked, the idea that they can be activated and actualized by the originations and existences of other conditions insinuates that there is something akin to *sabhāva* (self-nature) in each of them. Such self-nature persists as a mediating drive that rewrites the code of each formational instant. Historically, this idea was developed by the Yogachara/Yogācāra scholars, also known as Chittamatra/Citttamātra (Consciousness or Manifestation-Only). Yogācāra practitioners believe that their philosophical system was first proposed by Metteyya/Maitreya, a bodhisattva (enlightened sentient being) who now resides in the inner court of a universe called Tusita/Tuṣita. Historically, the scholar Asaṅga and his half-brother Vasubandhu (*c.* fourth–fifth centuries CE) are considered the founders of this school of thought, which, according to Yin Shun, most likely took concepts from the Sarvāstivāda. Their ideas were then further debated by their disciples Buddhasimha (dates unknown) and Dignāga (*c.* 480–540 CE). Their works were then revised by a new generation of scholars, among whom Sthiramati (475–555 CE) and Dharmapāla (530–61 CE) became the most discussed ones among Tibetan and Chinese scholars. The popularity of Yogācāra Buddhism, however, began to decline around the time of Dharmakīrti (*c.* sixth–seventh centuries), due to an ontological debate on monism.[19]

For Yogācāra scholars, forms that are constituted by dependent originations are called nominal or virtual existences, whereas the layouts — including their processes of becoming — of these dependent originations are called actual existences. For convenience, we can think about this distinction in semiological terms: (1) *paroles* (speech), as instantiations of differences, exist nominally; (2) a *langue* (language system), as a system of differences or a set of relations that are fundamentally empty, exists in actuality.[20] It is important to note that virtuality and actuality are interdependent, synchronic and relative to each other. Yogācāra scholars therefore treat them as shifting signifiers until they arrive at a point where their structural difference is rendered purposeless.

Perceptually and conceptually, the origination and existence of forms can be traced back to the operation of the six consciousnesses, which depends on the *ālambana-pratyata* (foundational condition) – that is, naming and constituting internal and external forms. According to Dignāga, what we call a *viññāna/vijñāna* (consciousness) is also a *vijñapti* (manifestation or representation). The governing potentiality or impetus that enables the origination and existence of seeing (i.e. sensing, perceiving and recognizing) is called *darśana bhāga* (potential to see). The origination and existence of this potential is dependent on the origination and existence of the *nimitta bhāga* (potential to generate signs). In the operation of the six consciousnesses, the originations and existences of acts of seeing and the signs being seen are confirmed by the *svasaṃvedana/svasaṃvitti* (potential to take the act of seeing and the signs being seen as self-evident, or self-reflexiveness).[21] Dharmapāla argues that *svasaṃvedana* can be further subcategorized into the potential to perceive and conceptualize a consciousness as self-evident, and the potential to generate a self-evident consciousness.[22]

According to Yogācāra scholarship, a consciousness can therefore be defined as an interdependent relationship between a potential condition and a being-conditioned condition. In Deleuzian terms, the potential condition is regarded as the virtual, whereas the being-conditioned condition is seen as the actual. Xuanzang (602–64 CE), who travelled from Chang'an (nowadays Xi'an) to Nalanda to study with Sthiramati and Dharmapāla, often simplified this relationship as one between the *xin* (minds) and *xiang* (perceptions). For him, the objective representation of *xiang* is called *jing* (milieu or image). In the *Cheng weishi lun* [*Vijñapatimātratāsiddhi*, or *Discourse on the Perfection of Consciousness-Only*], Xuanzang therefore argues that *yiqie fa cong xinxiang sheng* (the originations of all dharmas [phenomena] depend on the dependent originations between the minds and perceptions).[23]

The discrete dependent originations and existences of the six consciousnesses are perceptually and conceptually unified by *manas* (volition). The relationship between the potential to perceive and conceptualize volition and the potential to represent it as the self is called the *manas*-consciousness (volition-consciousness). Yogācāra scholars call this the seventh consciousness.

At this point, it is important to remind ourselves that all the dependent originations we have encountered thus far are synchronic. In other words, in a single *kṣaṇa*, a system of differences is instantiated as: (1) the actualization of potentialities and the virtualization of actualities; (2) the unification of the discrete operation of the six consciousnesses by volition and the proliferation of volition into the six consciousness-in-operation; (3) the dependent originations and existences between the potentiality to see and the potentiality to generate signs, and between the potential to perceive and conceptualize self-evidentiality and the potential to generate self-evident consciousnesses; (4) the dependent originations and existences between the minds and perceptions, and between these perceptions and their objective representations; (5) the mutual dependency between origination and extinction, existence and non-existence. While origination and existence are dependent upon the actualization of potentialities, extinction and non-existence are dependent upon the virtualization of actualities. In Sarvāstivāda terms, forms in turn function as seed conditions, which are formless and unmarked. They are deposited into a layout of potentialities called the *ālaya*-consciousness (storehouse consciousness). In this light, potentialities and conditions are mutually dependent, so as their layouts — that is, the *ālaya*-consciousness and the six consciousnesses, or, some say, the *ālaya*-consciousness and the volition consciousness.[24]

The mutual dependency between the *ālaya*-consciousness and the six consciousnesses enables potentialities and conditions to proliferate interdependently ad infinitum. For Yogācāra scholars, as actualizations and representations of the *ālaya*-consciousness, the six consciousnesses and the volition consciousness that summon them as a unity exist in name only. In other words, the only *thing* that actually exists is the *ālaya*-consciousness, a layout of potentialities that are formless, unmarked and dormant. As the *Saṃdhinirmocana Sūtra* [*Sutra of the Explanation of the Profound Secrets*] argues, the *ālaya*-consciousness can be understood as the ultimate *sabhāva* (self-nature) of all consciousnesses and manifestations, which is characterized by its *nihsvabhāvatā* (self-nature-less-ness).[25]

Fyodor Stcherbatsky argues that as a layout of potentialities, the *ālaya*-consciousness is timeless. Hence, to imagine that the infinite proliferation of potentialities and conditions takes place in one *kṣaṇa* is merely an analogy. For him, this timeless layout is conceptualized by Henri Bergson as the *durée*, an overall layout of duration upon which individuated originations and existences take place.[26] Once being represented as forms, they are perceived and conceptualized as a process of becoming consisting of an ever-operating *saṃsāra* (cycle).[27] In each *kṣaṇa*, a *saṃsāra* would produce a *sati/smṛti* (mindfulness or awareness). The origination and existence of one awareness is followed by another cycle of origination and existence in immediate contiguity, a sequence that would be perceived and conceptualized as a temporally continuous process of mediation.

Unlike the Sarvāstivāda scholars, Yogācāra thinkers do not propose that potentialities directly mediate the process of dependent originations. Rather, the seven consciousnesses, as a representation of the *ālaya*-consciousness, are conceived as a chronological sequence of actualization and virtualization, a process of *modulation* from one point-instant to another, which generates a sequence of awarenesses laid out in duration. Meanwhile, these modules are *perceived* as a perpetually operating cycle or process of becoming. It is on the level of perception that dependent originations can be regarded as a process of mediation between actualization and virtualization. This process of imaging is instantiated by a layout of forms and a code by which the origination, existence and extinction of these forms are written and rewritten in accordance to those changes in the layout itself. Thus, imaging is ultimately a form of imagination — and vice versa.

Long Day's Journey into Night

In this sense, what Gilles Deleuze calls the movement-image can be considered a karma-image, which refers to neither a particular mode of narration nor a mode of technical existence (e.g. celluloid film, television or digital media).[28] Rather, in Buddhist terms, it refers to the operation of the eight consciousnesses driven by karma. Such operation is instantiated in various technical forms, which constitute different modes of anthropotechnical existences and engagements. Karmic impulses propel modulations of conditions, from one *kṣaṇa* to another, which give rise to forms, sensations and affections, perceptions and conceptions, a cycle of initiation and extinction, and awarenesses and consciousnesses. Such *saṃsāra* constitutes what we call the cinema. Indulging in karma, these awarenesses initiate afflictions: avarice, frustration and anger, delusion, arrogance, suspicions, worries, sorrows, sufferings and anxieties. It confirms the existence of *manas*, the existential values of all forms, and an attachment to those pleasures and sufferings that constitute the ontological consistency of *my* existence and the existence of the milieu in which *I* dwell as *my* possessions. In other words, karmic impulses make imaging and imagination indiscernible.

Such indiscernibility is written into the textual structure and the cinematic experience of Bi Gan's *Long Day's Journey into Night*. This film is about a loner, Luo Hongwu (Huang Jue), who returns to his hometown, Kaili, to attend his father's funeral. In the first part of the film, he discovers a worn-out black-and-white photograph of a young woman inside a broken and rusted clock in an abandoned and gradually flooding miner dormitory where his parents used to live. Yet, the face of the woman is obscured by a cigarette burn on the image. The film indicates that this is a photograph of either his mother, Xiaofeng, and/or his first love, Wan Qiwen, a young woman who looks/looked like Xiaofeng and who used to be the girlfriend of his best friend, Wildcat, after his death. Behind this old photograph, someone has inscribed the name and phone number of a person, Tao Zhaomei, which triggers his desire to look for Qiwen.

This first section, which lasts seventy-nine minutes, is presented in 2D. The textual substratum of this section is Hongwu's journey to locate Qiwen. This continuous trajectory, however, is assembled by a series of fragmented memories of his romantic vignettes with Qiwen (Tang Wei) and of his friendship with Wildcat (Lee Hong-chi). These memories are then intercut with Hongwu encountering a young woman who resembles Qiwen, and therefore, his mother (also played by Tang Wei). The distinction between memories and Hongwu's lived reality in the present is not signalled textually or formally; rather, it is indicated very subtly by how grey his hair is, which is often obscured by the film's dim lighting and its monotone production design. Moreover, under such design, each frame is saturated with two primary additive and subtractive colours, which overwhelm the spectator's sensorium. Yet, the dim light softens their competition and turns these colours into a comforting, sleep-inducing and dreamlike assemblage of optical wavelengths. In other words, this first section of the film can be seen as an avalanche of awarenesses that are actualized from the seeds of an *ālaya*-consciousness, as a dominant condition (the cinematic apparatus) enables these potentialities to be imaged and imagined by Hongwu and the apparatus itself. These actualizations are driven by a series of karmic impulses, from one moment to another. What is absent, however, is a singular volition that organizes these spatiotemporally discrete moments into a coherent whole. In other words, it is unclear who is imagining/imaging. Therefore, the spectators are expected to become mindful of the connections between seed conditions and their matching conditions, when there is no clue in the text or form to indicate their mutual dependency and contiguity.

Figures 1 and 2. *Diqiu zuihou de yewan/Long Day's Journey into Night* (Bi Gan, 2018).

In one sequence, Hongwu manages to locate a middle-aged woman in prison, whom he believes to be Tai Zhaomei. In an over-the-shoulder medium close-up of this woman, we see Hongwu asking her if she is Zhaomei. After her denial, the camera dollies to the left slightly to give us a more frontal view of Zhaomei's face (Figure 1). In this shot, Zhaomei is seen through a piece of wired glass. She wears a clean blue uniform and sits against a nebulous green background under a pristine white light. She therefore appears to be an uncannily lifelike image in a damp, foggy and dreamlike milieu. Suddenly, this woman speaks *as* Zhaomei and recounts a story of her and Qiwen stealing the book that Hongwu is holding. This woman claims that she and Qiwen read the whole novel and that the poem in it could make a room spin. This sudden shift in this woman's identity in the scene makes visible and tangible how identities, memories and histories are intersubjectively configured as a perceptual-conceptual configuration. This confession appears to Hongwu and the spectators as an image, yet this image, as a perceptual-conceptual configuration, is also an actualized imagination.

Towards the end of this first section, we see Hongwu visiting Wildcat's mother in her salon. Here, Wildcat's mother looks content and relaxed, and she recounts how she taught Hongwu and Wildcat to dye her clients' hair. She laughingly tells Hongwu that no client would ever want to dye their hair pink. We then see Hongwu visiting an abandoned town and entering a cinema watching a film called *Long Day's Journey into Night*. Once he sits down, he puts on a pair of 3D glasses. As instructed by the usher prior to the screening, the spectators also put on their own. What follows in the next fifty-nine minutes is framed as a film within a film and a dream (imagination). This entire sequence, shot in a single long take, can be understood as a projection of Hongwu's/spectators' memories from the *ālaya*-consciousness onto the cinematographic body as a shared imagination between them. Yet, this shared imagination is projected, in all its reality and concreteness, as a continuous image in which both Hongwu and the spectators dwell.

This long take begins with Hongwu wandering to the back of the cinema (a cave), where he cannot find an exit. Instead, he meets a young man who recalls to Hongwu/the spectators the memory of Wildcat. This young man shows him an exit out of the cave and gives him a ping pong paddle which is supposed to enable him to fly. From the mountain, Hongwu takes an industrial cable cradle to descend slowly into a pinball machine parlour/pool hall located on a cliff overlooking a village. In the pool hall, he meets Kaizhen (also played by Tang Wei). As Kaizhen is harassed by a group of teenagers, Hongwu comes to her rescue. In revenge, the teenagers lock Kaizhen and Hongwu up in the pool hall. Hongwu then spins the ping pong paddle. At this point, the camera becomes one with Hongwu's and Kaizhen's bodies, which fly slowly down into the village. When the camera lands, it separates itself from Hongwu and Kaizhen and resumes its role as an observer and a follower.

Hongwu then wanders into a carnivalesque open-air karaoke, where he re-encounters Kaizhen backstage. Kaizhen is eager to show

Hongwu a room that belongs to a married couple, which is decorated like a fairy tale. However, Hongwu leaves Kaizhen backstage in an attempt to find Qiwen. As he returns to the karaoke, he then sees Wildcat's mother wearing a pink wig. She appears to be in distress, and she lights up a torch from a bonfire in the karaoke (Figure 2). After waving her torch against a few customers, she wanders down a series of steps in an attempt to convince a man to take her away from the village. Hongwu catches her in front of a gate as she begs the man behind the gate to take her away, and she does not recognize Hongwu.

After helping Wildcat's mother to escape with the man, Hongwu returns to Kaizhen backstage. Kaizhen then brings Hongwu to an abandoned and half-demolished living room, which she claims to be the bedroom of a pair of lovers. In this darkly lit room that is both visually and sensually 'dampened' by a wet and cold greyish blue, Kaizhen tells Hongwu that she has once heard from someone that this room will rotate if one knows the password. Hongwu then recites the poem from the book he held when he visited the prisoner, which makes the room spin. The camera then follows the rotating movement of the room and departs from Hongwu and Kaizhen. It then lands on the backstage of the karaoke. There, we see a brightly lit vanity with an orange tint and a lit Roman candle.

Like the production design and lighting in the first section of the film, these competing colours in the frame posit the spectators in a sensorially stimulating yet sleep-inducing milieu. In this milieu, time seems to flow continuously (in a long take). Yet, characters and events are generated and extinguished in this temporal continuum in a haphazard manner, thus foregrounding the fact that such a continuum is constituted by an assemblage of interdependently related yet mutually discrete reactivated seeds, which generate desire, frustration and delusion. The moving camera sometimes follows the characters and other times substitutes their bodies. As a result, the spectators, whom the camera is supposed to embody, *inhabit* this milieu neither as subjects nor objects, followers nor protagonists. Rather, the interdependent relationship between their bodies and the milieu are continuously and fluidly reconfigured and redefined in this drawn-out process of imaging-imagining — all driven by a series of karmic impulses from one moment to another. However, the indiscernibility between subject and object, and imaging and imagining, makes the spectators mindful of the process of becoming of all the dependent originations that constitute the image/imagination, thus drawing their attention to the operation of the consciousnesses itself and the karmic impetus that vocates, and is vocated by, each moment of such operation.

Conclusion

For Mahayana philosophers, the *ālaya*-consciousness, by default, operates perpetually with no beginning and no end. The operation of the *ālaya*-consciousness, from which all awarenessess are projected, is often compared to the image in a mirror, which has no existential value — that is, it is an imagination. This imagination, however, cannot be generated unless there is a permanent and timeless *image* that remains indifferent to the process of imagining. Yet, this surface does not have any fundamental nature or form. In this sense, the image *is* an imagination, whereas an imagination *is* the image. In this sense, as the *Vajracchedikā Prajñāpāramitā Sūtra* indicates, all phenomena or forms are like a dream or an illusion, an imagination that has no existential value, yet we cannot help but give them an imagistic substratum and regard them as *existent*. Meanwhile, they are like a dew drop or a flash of lightning — that is, they are impermanent — yet we cannot help but perceive them as continuous. This is what Buddhist philosophy calls *tathātā* — thusness, or the way it is.

NOTES

1   Nan Huai-chin, *The Diamond Sutra Explained* (lectures given in 1980; transcriptions first published in 2001), translated by Hue En (Pia Giammasi) (Florham Park, NJ: Primordia Media, 2003), §32, 303.

2   Christian Metz, 'The Imaginary Signifier', translated by Ben Brewster, *Screen* 16:2 (Summer 1975), 51.

3   All Buddhist terms are given in Pāli/Sanskrit, unless the term is pronounced the same way in both languages.

4   Huang Jiashu, *Za ahan jing daodu* [*Saṃyuktāgama:* A reading guide], *sūtras* translated by Guṇabhadra (1999; reprinted by Taipei: Buddhall, 2006), SA-1–7 (235–56), 11 (262–3), 58 (264–7), 68 (278–9), 262 (281–5), 274 (292–3), 297 (295–6), 309 (299–300), 319 (302), 322 (304–5), 335 (308–9), 1171 (315–17) and 1173 (319–22).

5   Regarding the dating of the *Saṃyuktāgama*, see Sujato, *A History of Mindfulness: How Insight Worsted Tranquillity in the* Satipaṭṭhāna Sutta (2012; reprinted, Taipei: Buddha Education Foundation, 2012), 31–6. Regarding the definition of dependent originations, see Huang, *Za ahan jing daodu*, SA-298 (178). My translation here refers to the definition of this phrase offered

by Yen P'ei, 'Genben bupai Fojiao yuanqi guan suo zhankai de qiji' [The turning point of the theory of dependent originations proposed by early sectarian Buddhisms], in *Fojiao de yuanqi guan* [On the concept of *nidānas* in Buddhism] (1981; reprinted, Taipei: Tianhua chuban shiye, 1997), 34.

6   Wei Yin, 'Fojiao de yinguo lun' [Buddhist theory of dependent originations], in *Fojiao zhexue sixiang lunji* [Anthology of critical essays on Buddhist philosophy], edited by Chang Man-t'ao (Taipei: Dasheng wenhua chubanshe, 1978), 1:218.

7   Aristotle, *Aristotle's Metaphysics*, translated by Joe Sachs (1999; reprinted, Santa Fe: Green Lion Press, 2002), XII, 1072a.

8   V. V. Kobychev and S. B. Popov, 'Constraints on the Photon Charge from Observations and Extragalactic Sources', *Astronomy Letters* 31;3 (2005), 147–51; Matthew D. Schwartz, *Quantum Field Theory and the Standard Model* (Cambridge: Cambridge University Press, 2014), 66.

9   Chi Fa, 'Yinyuan lun' [On dependent originations], in *Fojiao genben wenti yanjiu* [Studies of the fundamental questions in Buddhism], edited by Chang Man-t'ao (Taipei: Dasheng wenhua chubanshe, 1978), 1:87 and 95–6; Yen P'ei, 'Genben bupai Fojiao yuanqi guan suo zhankai de qiji', 45.

10   Chi Fa, 'Yinyuan lun', 88.

11   Huang, Za ahan jing *daodu,* SA-293 (326–7), 296 (330–2), 300 (337–8), 364 (341–2), 373 (344–6), 388 (348) and 404 (353–4); Asaṅga, *Yujiashi di lun* [*Yogācārabhūmi-śāstra,* or *Discourse on the Stages of Yogic Practice*], translated by Xuanzang (Taipei: The Buddha Educational Foundation, 2014), *juan* 9:16–20 (1:321–9); Nāgārjuna, *Dazhidulun* [*Mahāprajñāpāramitāśāstra* or *Great Treatise on the Perfection of Wisdom*], translated by Kumārajīva (Taipei: Shihua guoji gufen youxian gongsi, 2007), *juan* 5:35–6 (233–4); Fyodor Stcherbatsky, *Buddhist Logic* (1930–2) (1993; reprinted, Delhi: Motilal Banarsidass Publishers, 2008), 1:119–45.

12   Kaṇukurunde Ñāṇananda, *Concept and Reality in Early Buddhist Thought: An Essay on* Papañca *and* Papañca-Saññā-Saṅkhā (1971) (Sri Lanka: Dharma Grantha Mudrana Bhāraya, 2012), 5–6; Yin Shun, *Zhongguan lunsong jiangji* [Lectures on the Mūlamadhyamakakārikā] (1952; reprinted, Taipei: Zhengwen chubanshe, 2014), 277.

13   Ñāṇananda, *Concept and Reality*, 5–6.

14   See note 11.

15   Metz, 'The Imaginary Signifier', 48–50.

16   Vivian Sobchack, 'What My Fingers Knew: The Cinesthetic Subject, or Vision in the Flesh' in *Carnal Thoughts: Embodiment and Moving Image Culture* (Berkeley: University of California Press, 2004), 53–84.

17   See the *Kathāvatthu* [Points of controversy, dated *c.* 240 BCE], edited by Arnold C. Taylor (London: Pali Text Society by H. Frowde, 1894–7), Book XII, 264–71.

18 See the *Shelifu Apitan lun* [Śāriputrābhidharma-śāstra], in *Taishō Shinshū Daizōkyō* 25, no. 1548, §15 (144) and §25 (217).

19 Hong Xue, *Weishixue gailun* [Consciousness-only studies: A general introduction] (Chengdu: Bashu chubanshe, 2016), 8–23; Stcherbatsky, *Buddhist Logic*, 1:31–47; Yin Shun, *Shuo yiqieyou bu weizhu de lunshu yu lunshi zhi yanjiu* [A study of the *śāstras* and philosophers of and related to the Sarvāstivāda] (Taipei: Zhengwen chubanshe, 1968).

20 Ferdinand de Saussure, *Écrits de linguistique générale* (Paris: Éditions Gallimard, 2002), 25–45 and 82–3.

21 Dignāga, *Wuxiang si chen lun* [On the formlessness of sense data] in *Chen Na si lun* [The four *śāstras* by Dignāga], translated by Xuanzang (Nanjing: Zhina neixueyuan, 1932), 1:*Wu*:1–4.

22 Dharmapāla, *The Netti-pakaraṇa: With Extracts from Dhammapāla's Commentary*, edited by E. Hardy (London: Published for the Pali Text Society by Luzac, 1961).

23 Xuanzang, *Cheng weishi lun* [*Vijñapatimātratāsiddhi*, or *Discourse on the Perfection of Consciousness-Only*], in *Taishō Shinshū Daizōkyō* 31, no. 1585, §1 (1–2).

24 See notes 17, 21 and 23.

25 *Jie shenmi jing* [*Saṃdhinirmocana Sūtra*, or *Sūtra of the Explanation of the Profound Secrets*], translated by Xuanzang (Putian: Guanghua si, 2010), §4 (138).

26 Stcherbatsky, *Buddhist Logic*, 1:115–18, 436–9 and 482–6; Henri Bergson, *L'Évolution créatrice* (1907) (Geneva: Éditions Albert Skira, 1940), 19–24.

27 Stcherbatsky, *Buddhist Logic*, 1:183.

28 Gilles Deleuze, *Cinéma 1. L'image-mouvement* (1983; reprinted, Paris: Les Éditions de Minuit, 2015).

Notes on Contributors

Sarah Cooper is Professor of Film Studies at King's College London. Her books include *Selfless Cinema? Ethics and French Documentary* (Legenda, 2006); *Chris Marker* (Manchester University Press, 2008); *The Soul of Film Theory* (Palgrave-Macmillan, 2013); and *Film and the Imagined Image* (Edinburgh University Press, 2019). Her current research is on flowers and film.

Victor Fan is Senior Lecturer in Film Studies, King's College London and Film Consultant of the Chinese Visual Festival. His articles have appeared in journals including *Camera Obscura*, *Journal of Chinese Cinemas*, *Screen* and *Film History: An International Journal*. His books include *Cinema Approaching Reality: Locating Chinese Film Theory* (University of Minnesota Press, 2015) and *Extraterritoriality: Politics and Hong Kong Media* (Edinburgh University Press, 2019). He also makes films: his film *The Well* was an official selection of the São Paolo International Film Festival; it was also screened at the Anthology Film Archives, the Japan Society and the George Eastman House.

Albertine Fox is Lecturer in French Film at the University of Bristol, and her research is concerned with listening spaces in French and francophone documentaries, with a focus on the documentary convention of the filmed interview. Albertine has recently published three articles on Chantal Akerman's films and installations, including the documentary *De l'autre côté* (2002), the installation *Maniac Shadows* (2013) and the short film *Trois strophes sur le nom de Sacher* (1989), exploring Akerman's musical collaboration with Sonia Wieder-Atherton. Albertine's first monograph, *Godard and Sound: Acoustic Innovation in the Late Films of Jean-Luc Godard*, was published in 2017 by I. B. Tauris.

Abraham Geil is Senior Lecturer in Film Studies at the University of Amsterdam and a research fellow at the Amsterdam School of Cultural Analysis (ASCA). He is the co-editor of *Memory Bytes: History, Technology and Digital Culture* (Duke University Press, 2004) and has

Paragraph 43.3 (2020): 381–383
DOI: 10.3366/para.2020.0347
© Edinburgh University Press
www.euppublishing.com/para

published recent articles in *Polygraph*, *World Picture* and *Screen*. He is currently finishing a book on the uses and abuses of the human face as a privileged site of recognition in film theory for the Film Theory in Media History series at the University of Amsterdam Press.

Julian Hanich is Associate Professor of Film Studies and Head of the Department of Arts, Culture and Media at the University of Groningen. He is the author of *The Audience Effect: On the Collective Cinema Experience* (Edinburgh University Press, 2018) and *Cinematic Emotion in Horror Films and Thrillers: The Aesthetic Paradox of Pleasurable Fear* (Routledge, 2010). With Daniel Fairfax he recently co-edited *The Structures of the Film Experience by Jean-Pierre Meunier: Historical Assessments and Phenomenological Expansions* (Amsterdam University Press, 2019); with Christian Ferencz-Flatz he was responsible for an issue of *Studia Phaenomenologica* on 'Film and Phenomenology' (2016). His research focuses on film and imagination, cinematic emotions, film phenomenology, the collective cinema experience, and film style.

Robert Sinnerbrink is Associate Professor of Philosophy at Macquarie University, Sydney. He is the author of *Terrence Malick: Filmmaker and Philosopher* (Bloomsbury, 2019), *Cinematic Ethics: Exploring Ethical Experience through Film* (Routledge, 2016), *New Philosophies of Film: Thinking Images* (Continuum, 2011) and *Understanding Hegelianism* (Acumen, 2007; Routledge 2014), and is a member of the editorial board of the journal *Film-Philosophy*. He has published articles in journals such as the *Australasian Philosophical Review*, *Angelaki*, *Film-Philosophy*, *NECSUS: European Journal of Media Studies*, *Projections: The Journal of Movies and Mind*, *Post-Script*, *Screen*, *Screening the Past* and *SubStance*.

Jane Stadler teaches film and television studies at The University of Queensland, Australia, where she holds an adjunct position. She led a collaborative Australian Research Council project on landscape and location in Australian cinema, literature, and theatre (2011–2014) and co-authored *Imagined Landscapes: Geovisualizing Australian Spatial Narratives* (2016). She is author of *Pulling Focus: Intersubjective Experience, Narrative Film and Ethics* (2008) and co-author of *Screen Media* (2009) and *Media and Society* (2016). Her recent research focuses on ethics and the audience's affective responses to cinema.

Saige Walton is a Senior Lecturer in Screen Studies at the University of South Australia. She is the author of *Cinema's Baroque Flesh: Film,*

Phenomenology and the Art of Entanglement (Amsterdam University Press, 2016). Her articles appear in journals such as *Culture, Theory and Critique, NECSUS, Projections, Screening the Past* and the *New Review of Film and Television Studies*. Her current book project deals with the embodiment and ethics of a contemporary cinema of poetry.